SENSE OF DIRECTION

SENSE
OF
DIRECTION

The Director and his Actors

JOHN FERNALD

author of *The Play Produced,*
Destroyer from America

London
**SECKER AND
WARBURG**
[1968]

First published in England 1968 by
Martin Secker & Warburg Ltd
14 Carlisle Street, London W1

Copyright © 1968 by John Fernald

SBN: 436 15280 0

Printed in Great Britain by
Clarke, Doble & Brendon Ltd
Cattedown, Plymouth

Contents

Contents

for Jenny and Karin
in great gratitude

Preface

SENSE OF DIRECTION is a vital quality of exciting theatre. It conducts the audience towards a definite goal. But it is characteristic of theatre, in which duality intriguingly abounds, that *sense of direction* also means something else— the instinct for the craft possessed by him (once called in England the 'producer', but now fairly universally known as the 'director') who actually *directs* the process of making a performance come to life upon a stage. For me this is the most satisfying, the most rewarding activity imaginable, and I have long wanted to write about it. I have the notion—and it provides perhaps as useful an excuse for work as any—that there is, somewhere in the Platonic empyrean an ideal actor's re-creation of a character and an ideal performance of a play : these actually exist and have their being, if only somehow one can reach up and grasp them tight. Yet their origins are no more than a lot of words and instructions on a printed page. To attempt to reach this ideal in the theatre has been my professional duty for the past thirty-nine years. Naturally, I have never reached it (though I think there have been one or two people who have). My many attempts, however, have been rich in discoveries about the hazards and fascinations involved in the effort.

Although *acting* has been defined, in a curious and very British manner through the verdict of a minor court of law, as a 'Fine Art', 'Theatre' seems to remain, semantically speaking, beyond the pale of art altogether, being often due to no more than a temporary alliance of different and sometimes conflicting activities, loosely and not always effectively harnessed towards a single end. Yet, in its happier manifestations Theatre's results are 'artistic', and people who are not actors but who can not unfairly be called artists of a kind devote their lives to it, putting its demands before those of property and friends and family in order to achieve it as well as they possibly can. These people live in a kind of a dream, which they are ever trying to turn into reality, and I suppose I am one of them.

In the course of my planning for this book, I came across some words by a wise and civilized writer that seemed to illuminate my purpose in writing it. Maurice Baring, in his *Lost Lectures or the Fruits of Experience*, says:

'The "dream and the business": these two words sum up the whole of English character and the whole of English literature. The dream finds its expression in our lyric poetry, and the practical instinct of the Englishman in literature speaks in that most English of all books *Robinson Crusoe*. In *Robinson Crusoe* you find the spirit of adventure treated with the utmost matter-of-factness, the same spirit of adventure that inspired the deeds of British seamen and the dreams of English poets.'

This seems to me to express very nicely the duality which I have mentioned, for theatre embraces both art and commerce and its processes are inevitably a matter of calculated practicality as well as of creative inspiration.

It is not the purpose of the following pages to dwell, except for a little, upon the Dream. The dream is to be taken for granted, and to write about it is not in any way to aid a director to make it tangible: it is to help those who strive to realize the dream that the book is written.

I have used a great many quotations, some of them long. Some are from Shakespeare, a few from Ibsen; many more (because he provides so many interpretative opportunities) are from Tchehov. There is but a sprinkling from the modern drama. This is not because I am not sympathetic to modern drama: I have deliberately avoided spreading the net over a wider field. If there is a profit to be gained by reading this book it will be by frequent reference to complete copies of the plays discussed in it. I have therefore restricted the dramatists to little more than half-a-dozen, and the plays that are dealt with can be found inside three or four actual volumes. Further, if the book is to acquire any continuance of utility, then the examples in it should be mostly from plays which have already stood the test of time.

The translation from Ibsen is by Una Ellis-Fermor and that from the French by Jenny Laird. All from the Russian is by J. P. Davis, whose translations of Tchehov remain for me the only ones which truthfully render that dramatist's easy and natural rhythms of speech. Some of what appears here has already been published in the *Journal* of the Royal Society of Arts, and I am most grateful to the Society for their permission to incorporate it here. Some has appeared in the *Sunday Telegraph*, to the Editor of which my thanks. I have also drawn upon sundry addresses and lectures to students of the Royal Academy of Dramatic Art.

Finally I would like to express my deepest gratitude of all to a rare multitude of actors and actresses of all kinds and all ages for what has been taught to me by their many brimming talents. Without them, and the delight and excitement of working with them, this book could never have been written.

I · Introducing the Director

PROBABLY LESS IS KNOWN, by people of reasonably catholic artistic interests, of what the Theatre Director is and what he does than is known about any other kind of interpretative artist. The glamorous light which envelops the actor—and even sometimes the dramatist, with a sort of unreal halo, is not so often turned on to the director, and this is as well. His work is exclusively concerned with what play and performers need *from him*, and any encouragement to his ego by the flattery of publicity can upset the delicate balance that must exist between him and his human material.

But before it can be explained what the director is, it must be stressed what he is *not*, for the public is, I think, befogged about him because of the way the newspapers tend on the whole to regard him. In general, the press holds him generally responsible for the visual aspects of a production, décor, lighting and 'effects' etcetera. For example, a glance at the notices of Peter Brook's famous Stratford production of *King Lear* with Paul Scofield will show that much emphasis was given to the fact that this production consisted visually of two vast metallic walls, which closed in or opened out, and which, bathed in a fairly unvaried and merciless white light, served for the whole gamut of Shakespeare's scenic universe. All this it was easy for the critic to describe and to criticize. What was not easy was for anybody who had not been present at all the rehearsals to divine how Peter Brook and Paul Scofield applied their own minds to Shakespeare's thinking, how they decided to present the sweep of his rhythms, and the counterpoint between speech and speech, where it was agreed that Lear's words have one meaning and perhaps the thought behind them a different meaning, how far the majesty of sonority and dynamics should be worked for, or how little, (since these qualities uphold keenness of intellectual expression only up to a point, after which acuteness of acting is blurred by its own noise). These questions, and countless others which must have arisen from them, will only have been answered after many weeks', perhaps many months' study of the play by its director. Yet they are nearly all of them outside the possibility of a critic's knowledge: he can at best refer to them briefly in the form of a personal opinion of the way the play is 'spoken'; more than that it is not easy for him to do. And so theatrical journalism confines itself in the main to dwelling upon those aspects of a production which (though they are undoubtedly in the domain of a director's responsibility) are superficial, most obvious, and most open to gimmickry, such as scenic novelty and effects of sound and light.

It so happens that these obvious quantities were also the ones most in evidence at the time when directors first began to be thought important—in Scandinavia in the nineties because of the plays of Ibsen, in Russia about the same time because of those of Tchehov, directed by Nemirovitch—Danchenko and Stanislavsky, and in France because of the theatre of Antoine. In England the cult of the director did not start properly till later. Even as late as the early twenties of this century it was possible to see in a London West End programme the legend 'The Play Stage-Managed by . . .' modestly set forth underneath the names of the cast. The individual designated was indeed the stage manager, but he was also the person who was responsible for grouping and lighting the production, and for disciplining and to some extent influencing the performances of the less important actors. The particular actor-manager concerned bore, however, the main artistic responsibility. But the great actor-managerships of Irving, Tree and their successors helped, with their own emphasis upon scenic effect, to perpetuate a false idea in the minds of critics, and therefore of the public which followed them, that 'production' (which they then called 'stage management', and which we now know as 'direction') was one thing, and 'acting' was something else and entirely unconnected with it.

This, of course, is nonsense. The true director is deeply concerned with acting and he is responsible for the kind of acting which occurs in the performance under his charge. The fact that he is also the ultimate arbiter over scenery, lighting and stage effects must not obscure the fact that the acting is more than 80 per cent of the performance.

The director stands towards his actors very much as the conductor of an orchestra towards his musicians. Every nuance of significance, of tone colour, of dynamics, of tempo, of contrasting and contrapuntal vocal effect—plus the containment of a continual stimulating variety within the discipline of an overall flow of rhythm and meaning—all this he must achieve through his actors. Anyone who has ever noticed, in radio programmes illustrating the subject, how many differing ways individual conductors tackle the same classical symphony—where the layman might be excused for imagining that a Beethoven or a Schubert could only be dealt with in two ways—either dully or excitingly—may perhaps appreciate that the same is true in drama. But one must not push the parallel of directors and orchestral conductor too far: there is one obvious and vitally important difference between the two. The discipline demanded of an orchestra by the conductor is complete and absolute: the player must and expects to play exactly as he is told. But the actor is, and must always be, an individualist seeking his own personal synthesis of his material with his imaginative and creative processes. And it is in the reconciling of the actor's individualistic vision with his own vision of the performance as a whole that the fascinations—and the pitfalls—of the director's work are apt to be found. In this too is the reason why some directors feel insecure—even when they appear to be successful.

Just as there were no such things as orchestral conductors in Bach's day, so once there were no theatre directors. Just as orchestras grew out of small ensembles of individual musicians playing together—the ensembles growing larger and larger as new kinds of tone colours began to be discovered through the invention of new musical instruments, until the conductor became a positive necessity in order that these new large forces could be co-ordinated and controlled—so the art of acting gradually grew beyond the point where it was best and solely practised in an individualistic way or by comparatively small groups. But the process in our Western European Theatre has been slow and by no means straightforward. There are particular differences between actors and musicians to account for this. Musical performers fall easily and tidily into two distinct kinds: those whose sole ambition is to be a perfect player; and those intensely individualistic ones who must be soloists or nothing. There is seldom any desire for musicians of the first group to see themselves as bettering themselves by entering the second group. And, noticeably, to many first-class musicians destined never to become household names, there is a special and rarified joy to be got out of playing with other people, which more than compensates for their comparative obscurity.

Not so with actors. Practically all actors are ingrained individualists—indeed egotists, and they can and will project their individuality on the slightest provocation and in the smallest parts if they get the opportunity. So, for the actor, the unselfish ensemble playing which is demanded by a certain type of play can be, though an invaluable discipline, also a source of constraint. The delight which can indeed be found in it is not immediately apparent, and only the most persuasive and subtle of directors can guide actors—more often than not with the actors themselves not recognizing the process—towards the haven of perfect balanced playing that he, the director, alone is actively seeking.

The question of the actor's intense individualism—a most

essential individualism, let me hasten to add, without which he would be no good at all—lies intriguingly behind all the director does. If the director allows it the full rein which its possessor would like, there is no hope whatsoever that he can achieve his aim to 'orchestrate' his script and transform what the dramatist has written on the page into performance. So a director must not give in to all his actor's desires. But neither must he fight these desires, for if he does his production will not be merely negative but a positive shambles. He has to take a lesson from that ancient Japanese art of combat, whereby the successful warrior has used his opponent's very strength to make him end up in a position he hadn't expected. So, he uses his actor's egotism to steer him by stealth and guile, and even flattery to some extent, to take the path he wishes him to take. And if the actor in the end believes that it is his own inclination that he is following, why then so much the better.

Until the late nineteenth century the physical conditions under which plays had to be performed held the development of subtlety and variety in acting in severe check. It was not until the revolution of scientific stage lighting made it possible for the first time for an actor to be *seen* thinking, and to *pause*, that variety of facial expression, for example, could become a factor in performance.

Elizabethan and Jacobean drama was played in daylight in the enclosed space of the wooden 'O', or else indoors by the feeblest of candle or oil illumination. The more efficient placing of illumination in the Restoration playhouses, while it shone more generously on the general action of a play, did nothing to bring out the actors' faces in relief and give prominence to what their expression was like.

What this must have meant for the actors must have been a general demand that they 'get on with it'—always flowing in word and deed, never stopping, or hardly ever, for the breather of a pause. For a pause could only have meant the snuffing out of all dramatic impetus and very great difficulty in regaining it. For the Elizabethan and Jacobean drama such unrelenting persistence could have seemed no loss: it suited the natural exuberance of the generally accepted verse form. What mattered was the spoken word, and of course it was taken completely for granted by all that the *entire* range of human feelings could be—and could only be—expressed by words alone. Hence the drama continued to be exclusively 'literary' throughout the seventeenth and eighteenth centuries and even in the greater part of the nineteenth. Even when 'literature drama' became debased, it was still exclusively through the handling of words—and the handling of them in a broad way—that playwrights and actors worked their magic with the audience. The actors' overwhelming technical problem must have been diction: they must have practised hard at getting their tongues over the hurdles of polysyllabic declamation, and there was surely not much about how to achieve breath reserve—necessary to sustain feeling and sense over lengthy flowing passages—that they did not know two hundred years ago. The coming of gas in the nineteenth century may well have begun to release the actor from the monotony of a steady flow of words: Macready could not have made his famous pauses without the glare of the lime-light. But subtlety of facial expression was surely still a long way off: over-bright white light wipes out detail in expression; moreover, as gas extended, the numbers of people who could see the actor at all increased, and consequently this allowed theatres to be larger. The bulk of the audience were scarcely better off than they were before.

There was still no need yet for anything that a *director* could do. No one could know better than the actor whether or not he was getting over to his audience. The experienced actor has a sixth sense which tells him if he loses touch for a single moment. The younger actor will learn this when the coughs and restlessness of a house which cannot hear properly has told him plainly enough. More and more, inevitably, the 'pyramid' built itself up—the hierarchy of star player, and supporting responsible players—together with the lesser breeds of beginners. More and more, too, did these gradually develop a remoteness from life and a general staginess of 'acting' that characterized the nineteenth-century theatre and which a few of us have even found oddly surviving into the twentieth. The inevitable disciplinarian of the company was its leader, the actor manager, and to quite an extent he taught those round him how to do their jobs better. But he taught them from a viewpoint which to us is false, for to put it simply, he was concerned, in interpretation, mainly with what influenced an audience and what did not: every happening was judged by this criterion—'was it effective, or wasn't it?' 'Effectiveness' was a criterion merely of itself, nothing more. But a world of difference separates what is just effective from what is imaginative, perceptive and true. How could the actor alone, from his isolated position on the stage, judge of such subtler values? The fact is, he was unable to do so, and from the moment when that greater range of values came to be found desirable and necessary, so the need for the theatre director was born.

By the third quarter of the nineteenth century the theatre had become solidly entrenched in a fustiness of traditional habit that removed it far from the feel of life. At the same time its practitioners had built a set of rules of what to do and not to do upon the stage, all based on experience of what was effective and what was not, that in their way are perfectly viable. It is possible for us still to get a flavour of what this sort of acting was like. There are gramophone records in which the voices of famous actors of the past are preserved, and a memorable one is that of Lewis Waller doing his version of _Henry_ V in 'Once more into the breach'. His was supposed at the time, I believe, to be a definitive _Henry_ V, yet the way he tackles the speech would seem to us today to have virtually nothing to do with true acting, as an Olivier or a Finney would understand the phrase, at all. The speech has a sweep of flow and a noble ring about it, but it seems to come from a world in which actors have some special way of pitching their voices and a general intonation which has nothing to do with life and a real personality. As if to live and behave in the world was one thing and 'acting' quite another. It seems that people accepted this division quite naturally as a matter of course and thought there was nothing odd about it. They accepted, too, odd quirks of personality which they found appealing—because a 'great personality' was so much part of being a 'great actor'—that phenomena like Henry Irving's extraordinary personal habits of pronunciation and emphasis, and Sir Johnston Forbes-Robertson's cosy avuncular and old gentlemanly Hamlet were taken perfectly for granted.

The great watershed which marked the change which was to come over the theatre, and immensely enlarge its horizon —and consequently to make the art of the director necessary —came with a new approach to dramatic writing which took place towards the end of the nineteenth century and at its turn. In Scandinavia Ibsen, in Russia Tchehov, in England Shaw, Granville-Barker and the Manchester playwrights—in all these places vastly differing talents and dramatic purpose began to have one particular effect, and this was, strangely enough, the liberation of the actor from the tyranny of the spoken word. An odd effect indeed, you might think, to spring from Ibsen or Shaw or Barker, in whom such a power of intellectual argument had been released by their very fluency of written thought. But the thing that all the new playwrights had in common, no matter how different their aims in other respects, was the fact that words became avenues to something beyond words. To ideas, to wide fields of exploration of human motives, and in the particular case of Tchehov to a deep-ranging exploration of human personality. Words were no longer the total enclosing means to express what the dramatist wanted to say.

The change was sweeping. Drama turned in a compara-tively short time from being narrative and 'linear' to being spatial and to an existence on several planes at once. This is not of course to underestimate the wondrous scope of the Elizabethan drama, or the achievements of the seventeenth- and eighteenth-century dramatists, but merely to point out that the nature of poetic and literary drama puts certain limits on a director's scope for 'orchestration': the more the literary drama degenerated, and the more it moved away from reality in the nineteenth century, the less need there could have been for the director's function.

Tchehov's discovery that words themselves hardly mattered at all, and that it was only what lay *between* the lines that mattered, was a revolution. It brought the director into being and transformed the art of acting. Here came the discovery of a storehouse of what I must call—for want of a better name—'theatrical values' which correspond to the musical values of the composer and musician and which give validity to the concept of the director as a sort of theatrical orchestral conductor. The pause for thought, the pause for suspense, the ejaculatory line immediately following a slower more flowing cadence, the contrast of pitch, tone and rhythm, the relation between the actor's movements, gestures and facial expression, the timing of everything he does—these and a host of similar things are to the director as musical notes and harmonies to the musician. And, just as to interpret the organic structure of a symphony is part of the conductor's task, so the director has to find and express the flowing shape of a drama which the author, interested quite possibly more in its content than in its form is himself unaware of. One can describe a director as someone whose instinct it is to seek out the pattern and the significance of the material, and to realize that the form and the content are different ways of looking at the same thing. The achievement, which without the director is not possible, is that of unity out of diversity.

Now for examples of what a director can do. The first, from Tchehov's early play *Ivanov*. Ivanov, a brilliant and vital landowner with progressive aspirations, has in him a demon of self-destruction which drives him to dissipate his energies into a state of nervous wreckage at the age of 35. His beautiful Jewish wife is dying of consumption, hastened by the knowledge that he has fallen romantically in love with the young Sasha Lebedyev, who worships him and believes that she can bring him back his lost youth. In the last act Ivanov, his wife now dead, is to be married to this determined girl: this catches all the characters at a moment of truth. Both Sasha and Ivanov realize too late that the marriage holds no future for either of them, but Sasha also knows that convention, propriety and civilized habit are too strong to let her break off a betrothal at the last moment. The momentum of the closing scene starts with Sasha confessing to her father that there is something wrong about Ivanov, and her father begging her not to go through with the marriage, and Sasha obstinately insisting that she must persevere all the same— which makes her fond old father throw up his hands in despair: Sasha's realization of her own obstinacy too brings her near to tears. Enter now two subsidiary characters: first Count Shabelsky, a broken-down poor relation of Ivanov's who has been shamelessly courting a rich parvenue widow for her money. The sudden sight of the 'cello which he used to play in duets with Ivanov's wife brings Shabelsky a realization of his worthlessness, and the shabbiness of his intrigue with the widow. He bursts into tears. Enter the widow herself, eager to develop a relationship with a man of noble birth. As soon as she sees him she sees he no longer wants her. She bursts into tears. Enter Sasha's mother, dressed for her daughter's wedding, sentimentally ready to cry at the slightest provocation because of the occasion. She bursts into tears. And there is Sasha's bewildered old father, not fully understanding what anything is about, standing in the middle of the stage, surrounded by three weeping women and one weeping old man. And into the middle of this there suddenly bursts Ivanov himself, somehow the cause at the bottom of everybody's trouble, come to demand of Sasha—twenty minutes before she is due to appear in church—that she call the wedding off.

Here are a set of inter-related situations each of which is a personal tragedy made inevitable by the effect of circumstances on character. Taken separately each is deeply moving, demanding the fullest extension of the actor's emotional powers. But Tchehov the compassionate interpreter of human suffering was also Tchehov the detached observer of the human comedy. Comedy can show itself as a set of recurring patterns—a rhythmic mechanism*—against the haphazard fluidity of ordinary life. The director must find the pattern if Tchehov's full flavour is to be brought out. It is not enough for each of the characters to act out their subjective emotions: the *relation* between them must be sought in theatrical terms. As each of the characters reach their tearful climax, so these are carefully graded to mount and to vary: Sasha's tears are controlled, Shabelsky's far less so, the widow's shallower, but wetter, the mother's wetter still, and as a measure of man's incomprehensibility of himself, Sasha's father's increasing bewilderment at it all marks the truth, that what seems tragic to ourselves, viewed closely, can be comic to other people, viewing the same thing from farther off. These scenes must be rhythmically tied together: the director must never lose sight of their total sum, though preserving the intensity and individuality of each individual moment. It is a matter of instinctive judgment to achieve this without which there can still be fine acting and memorable moments but no real performance in the fully realized sense.

What can the modern director, without presumption, do with Shakespeare, whose works were not written with his activities in mind? I have called Shakespeare's writing 'linear' because I suggest that in plays of his time plots unfolded in chronological order, and characters usually behaved and spoke as if they did not know what was going to happen to them in the future, however much they may have speculated. Now,

*See *Essay on Laughter* by Henri Bergson, Macmillan, New York, 1937.

imagine the effect of abandoning this 'linear' concept in a play such as *The Tempest*. Prospero is often regarded as something of a bore. Granted his sublime moments, he can still seem an unsympathetic figure as he tells Miranda the long story of his life, and particularly in his treatment of Ariel, Caliban and Ferdinand. It is a long time before the arrival of Gonzalo, and the Court, and the final explosion into comedy with Trinculo and Stephano. But what a difference there is when the 'linear' concept is abandoned! The opening of the play catches Prospero at the pinnacle of his power, the summit of his wisdom. '*By his art*' his enemies are at his mercy; at the '*sixth hour*' the moment will be at hand when his power and his wisdom will be put to the test. Yet, if he has become truly wise, '*neglecting worldly ends, all dedicated to closeness and the bettering of his mind*' then the revenge for which he has worked these twelve years simply must not, cannot happen. Usually Prospero does not realize the necessity of this abnegation until he is touched by Ariel's feeling for Gonzalo and the courtiers: and then the sudden change seems almost to betray all that he has stood for up to now as a determined justifier of himself. But what if Prospero has *always* known that the achievement of supreme power and wisdom must mean that that power has to be sacrificed, and the magic staff broken, at the very moment of consummation? What if the problem on Prospero's mind at the play's beginning is not just the confounding his enemies, but is the question of whether his human frailty can stand the test of the self-denial to which the logic of his '*art*' has brought him? In this light the play can be played, as far as Prospero is concerned, entirely differently. For over it hangs a question-mark, a turbulence in Prospero's mind, and a consequent theatrical suspense in the audience's: 'Will Prospero be equal, when the crisis comes, to the nobility to which he knows he should rise?' Over the recital of past events to his daughter, over his treatment of Ariel, of Caliban, even of Ferdinand, hang thunder clouds of doubt, of alternate power and impotence, as befits a man who is as yet still not sure of himself. And so, by a simple yet overwhelming change of viewpoint even the greatest of masterpieces can be illumined.

At this point we should consider a certain singularity about the director, and that is his relationship to his actors and to his author. This has none of the definition that we are used to in thinking about his cousin the conductor: as I have said, we cannot push the musical analogy too far. The director, it is usually true to say, begins with a company of performers who are in a state of wary anarchy. The actors are determined first of all to make certain that they will find their individual paths to the truth unimpeded. This makes a stage production an adventure, where the goal of artistic success is made the more worthwhile because it has to be earned by indirect means, subtly, and not just taken for granted. There is zest in this and it is something like the zest of the hunt in which the quarry is the getting of the actor to do what is wanted without his realizing that he is being worked upon. For the actor's aim and the director's are not the same. The lion of the theatre jungle is still the actor—still the king of beasts, who will rule supreme, director or no director. Yet it is true that theatre art is better served if the beast can be induced to perform according to a determined plan and pattern.

HEDDA: So he wasn't wearing vine leaves in his hair.....
BRACK: I beg your pardon?
HEDDA: Nothing. Go on.

To read these three lines aloud, with intelligence, takes five seconds: to perform them properly could take four times as long. Between 'I beg your pardon' and 'Nothing' lies a universe of significance—it can be truth or falsehood, depth or triviality, ruthlessness, remorse, regret, self-hatred, morbid sentimentality or all these things together—the combinations and contradictions of Hedda's feelings can seem endless in that pause before she answers. But it is not only the world of Hedda's feelings that we glimpse: if actress and director choose, time can stand still at this moment, and the plane of our own emotions intersects with that of hers. A beautiful woman has us in her power: our hearts beat with Hedda's, and we, the audience, submit willingly to a rhythm dictated by director and actress. Should she turn her head to answer we may admire how she does it. So we are totally engaged, partly within the thoughts and emotions of a fictitious character, partly with our own reactions, which are themselves part feeling, part appraisal of physical values exhibited by a body and a personality. There is an unescapable duality in the art of performance: there is endless multiplicity in the spectrum of human consciousness which it can reveal both in what a dramatist has created and in ourselves.

Such discoveries are there to be made between the lines and words of any creative dramatist after Ibsen—and of even the most modest of work-a-day playwrights. What can be discerned within the written sense itself is simple by comparison. Both worlds of significance, the unwritten and the written, are the worlds explored by the interpretative artist, the actor and the director, and it is here that the director can most easily betray himself and fail in his responsibility. Anybody can read a play and tell you what the writer's words 'mean'. The director, however, with his actors, discovers what lies behind them (and what lies behind them can, surprisingly, often be nuances and even significances of which the writer himself is not and has never been aware).

The director lies at the intersection of several lines of communication between those who create and those who receive what is created. First, the conception of the dramatist: the director must convey the totality of the author's intention—that goes without saying. This involves far more than merely expressing all that has been written in the script. The way he deals with this will emerge in later chapters, but here it should be said that as often as not the director must protect an author against himself. A dramatist is nearly always over-fond of all that he has written and forgets that a director and his actors will be able to 'say' many things without using any words at all. Whenever a pause or a gesture or a movement can be used instead of words, words become superfluous. The director will have to convince the author that this is true : so he must, amongst other things, be a diplomatist, under-standing people in life as well as people on paper.

He must understand his actors both as artists and techni-cians and as people, working with them for the ends of the finished product. This is not easy, because as I have already said, their aims are not necessarily the same as his, The director seeks a performance of a composite entity, while actors seek the creation and expression of their individual characterizations. A director can and should help them in this, and the more he understands about the processes of the actor the more he will be able to do so. But if he does not understand enough, the actor will seek his path to perform-ance without him, while he, the director, will be looked upon as a mere encumbrance, and that particular line of force will by-pass him altogether, making it difficult if not impossible for him to fulfil the equally important function of blending the individual performances into the composite whole. (Actors *must*, because they are individualists playing individual characters, oppose any *conscious* attempt to force them into a mould : appeals to them to become part of a pattern therefore will inevitably fall on deaf ears. Directors *must*, because they are responsible for the total result, try to achieve their goal of balanced effect, and can therefore only do so by indirect means.)

Other lines of communication which the director may strengthen or stand aside from at his peril are those of the designer, the lighting expert and even, today, the theatre architect. All these experts are individualists and all of them are quite likely to be egocentric. None are by nature inclined to consider the whole and all have an exaggerated idea of the importance of their own contribution. The positive director who wants a result which will satisfy his own conscience must control these, otherwise they will control him, and possibly stultify all his efforts: scenery will overpower the play, actors will play their parts in and out of pools of shadow, and be neither properly seen nor properly heard. A director should never forget that of all contributors to a performance it is the actor who matters most.

What are the aims, the precedences, which should satisfy the conscience of a truthful director? First, he should feel happy to submerge his own ego in the interests of the whole. He is there first of all to serve his author and secondly to serve his actors. All his creative abilities must be harnessed to balancing the many forces which he can command so that what emerges is something *more* than the play itself, creatively interpreted by actors—in fact a *performance*. For him this thing which we call a performance is what justifies his existence, what makes a production by him different from a production by anyone else. It is a result achieved unobtrusively, not by dominating the actors, not by persuading them even, but by showing them paths to perceptions which inspire their own performances. Such paths are discovered by director and actors together, and the exploration is done, as it were, by a party of equals, in which the director leads the way, his leadership being justified not by his office but by the fact that it is he who makes most of the discoveries. If he cannot make them he must yield to others in the party who can (and if he has to yield too often he must reconcile himself to being merely director *ex officio*, functioning as a nominal authority in the field of costumes, scenery and lighting, as do many, in fact, who are 'directors' only in name). His leadership is exercised by clever strategy: where there are many 'paths' from which an actor might profitably choose, there is likely to be only one which the director-artist will feel is exactly right for his purposes, only one which satisfies his sense of pattern and unity. But he will not, if he is wise, appear to make his choice for those reasons which appeal to him most, since these reasons are quite unlikely to appeal to his actors: he must 'sell' his ideas to them in terms which will win their hearts. When the 'path' is eventually chosen, it has to seem the right one without reservations, to all concerned.

And so the good director must be someone who cares more about his results than about fame for himself. If his personality and his reputation are powerful enough he can, of course, dominate his actors completely and force them where he wills. In this way he can grow in power and become a subject for theatrical journalists to write about. But if he falls for this there is one thing of which he can be sure, and that is that the actors whom he has treated in this way will not give him the best of which they are capable. He will be in the position of a conductor who is brilliantly wielding an orchestra which has mysteriously become composed of second-class players. But if he will think only of the result, if he will seek satisfaction through the fulfilment of his cast, and enjoy the subtleties of leading them without them fully realizing that they are being led, then he can achieve (with good material) a true fulfilment for himself. He will discover that any manuscript of quality has its counterpart as a performance in his own imagination, and he will find his fulfilment in attempting and sometimes very nearly creating this platonic ideal upon the stage.

II · The Audience

THE DIRECTOR is there first of all to serve his author and secondly to serve his actors. Yet this is far from being the whole story, since both author and actor serve the *audience*, for whom they both exist. Without an audience there can be no theatre, and it is fruitful for the director to understand certain of its essential needs.

These needs exist whatever the level of taste or intellectual significance on which a play is written: what follows therefore is not concerned with 'good', 'bad', 'high brow' or 'low brow', true or meretricious. It is concerned with basic facts about the audience which the director ignores at his peril. First it must be realized that an audience has a *persona* of its own, and that this is only very slightly related to the qualities of the single persons who compose it. It reacts in the theatre at the mental and emotional pace of its slowest member, and not with the agility of any of its quicker-witted components. Its dominant characteristic is perhaps a certain lethargy (an audience of brilliant people, while quicker in the uptake than an audience of dullards, will still be surprisingly slow in its reactions). It brings its inertia with it into the theatre—and there it sits waiting for some sort of magic to sweep that lethargy away.

'Magic', I believe, is the right word; the success of the magician depends upon a knowledge unrealized by those under his spell, while the latter's reactions of wonder, excitement or fear are traditionally apt to happen in the solar plexus, rather than in the mind. (Mental activity does of

course occur in appreciation of theatre, if the play is intellec-
tually *demanding enough*. But the intellectuality of a play
is most savoured after seeing its performance : if mental effort,
beyond certain limits, is expected of an audience during the
performance, its concentration will not be equal to the task.
The individuals composing it might all of them enjoy a
Socratic dialogue in the study but, as an audience, be quite
incapable of following it on the stage.)

The magic used to stir the audience from its inertia is the
primitive cunning of the story-teller. The author of *Pinocchio*
knew exactly what he was doing when he began his famous
story (the italics are mine).

'Once upon a time' (*tension starts*) 'there was—' (*after the
pause, tension breaks into the pleasure of recognition*)
—'a king!' at once exclaim our little readers. 'No!
Children you are wrong.' (*Tension grows again, but more
than before, for something exceptional and unexpected
must clearly be coming.*) 'Once upon a time there was—'
(*tension grows further*) 'a piece of wood.' (*Surprise and
astonishment: then resolution of tension. But now, what
is coming next?*).

There is the basic pattern on which, with variants, the audience depends : tension, followed by resolution, followed by
tension again and another resolution; with the question-mark
increasing tension further, as soon as the prospect of an answer
is raised. The 'story' expressed by the pattern is really a series
of adventure stories. Tension, leading to excitement, points
to adventure : recognition and explanation bring the relief
of a 'return home', while with the question-mark comes the
call to fresh adventures. To a musician the pattern is instantly
recognizable as that of a simple song. A child listening to a
bed-time story reacts to it without knowing or caring why.
The audience is like the child.

It is in *how* things are said and done by *the actors* that
this basic pattern is expressed. To describe it is best done by

pointing out what happens when it is absent. We are most of us familiar with the technique of the professional hypnotist, whose object is deliberately to put his victims into a trance. He murmurs softly and steadily into the ear of his subject: his pace never varies, his voice never rises above a regular monotone, his matter is limited and repetitive—and in no time at all the subject finds himself asleep. That is where the theatre audience will also find themselves—unless the contrary technique is used. The audience, if they are to be kept awake, must be spoken to in a special way, which exploits all possible opportunity for variety, through differences of volume, pitch, tempo, etcetera, in the telling. But, more than that, the arrangement of these qualities—what I have called the *theatrical values*, analogous to the notes of the musician—must be arranged so that they create their own pattern of alternate tension and relaxation. That is the 'story' that they tell. The actor creates tension by a change of pitch or a change of tempo or a change of volume, or a pause, or by a movement. He resolves tension by a resumption to an earlier tone or speech—by a return to something like what he was saying or doing before.

This alternation is the basic rhythm of performance. It is as necessary to the audience as breath to life. The director quarries it out of the dialogue, and some of the ways he does this are discussed in the next chapter.

Meanwhile, there is another need of the audience, which is the direct consequence of its comparative slowness to react. The audience can only *fully* take in, and digest, *one theatrical effect at a time*. If two important moments are happening together, or close together, the 'stronger' of the two will survive, but it will do so in a blurred form, because its effect is dampened by the existence of the weaker. The audience here is trying to do what it cannot do—take in two ideas simultaneously: if two people speak at once it is almost impossible to take in what they say, and the same is true if they are both using their full power of expression at one and the same time. When performers A and B are praised for 'acting beautifully together' what is really happening is that A's efforts intermesh with B's so finely and so precisely that they *seem* to be acting 'together'. The audience's attention is first on A and then on B, and it is very necessary that B should remain comparatively quiescent while A has the point of attention, otherwise A's performance will suffer through the audience not concentrating fully upon it. It is at the moment when the point of attention is actually transferring itself from A to B and back again that the audience's *comparative* slowness has to be reckoned with. 'Comparative' is important here, because though the transference is as quick as lightning, it is far slower than it would be for an individual listening to people talking in real life. Here is a familiar moment from *The Cherry Orchard*:

ANYA: . . . how are things here? Has the interest been paid?

VARYA: How could it be?

ANYA: Oh dear, oh dear!

VARYA: The estate will be sold in August.

ANYA: Dear, dear!

LOPAHIN: (*looks in at the door, moos like a cow, and exits.*)

VARYA: (*through tears*) I should like to give it him! (*Shakes her fist at the doorway*)

ANYA: (*Quietly, as she embraces Varya*) Varya, has he proposed?

(*Varya shakes her head.*)

There is of course a very great deal behind the disarming simplicity of this dialogue. Anya and Varya are contrasted characters, the former, warm-hearted and impulsive, the latter introspective, shy and inclined to make heavy weather of life. Their lines cannot be spoken quite in the light trite way that would happen in life—although the *appearance* of this is what

B

the actresses will have to arrive at. The audience will need to understand not only what the girls say, but what they *are*. The earlier part of the scene has consisted of Anya's long story about her mother's goings on in Paris, and so the audience will have been thinking not of Anya but of Liouba. At this point the audience will have their first chance, after the hurly-burly of the family's arrival, to take in the girls' characters as they sit quietly together. Anya's first question about the interest is loaded with significance, though she must say it with the sympathetic lightness of her nature. The way she speaks must compel the audience to look at her—so that they may catch the substance behind that lightness. The question-mark leads the eye to Varya: to Varya there is no lightness about the matter, and she gives 'How *could* it *be*' its full weight. To do that it is useless for her to speak immediately, for if she does so while the point of attention is still on Anya her acting will be wasted, since the audience can only take in one effect at a time, and therefore no one will be watching her. A fractional moment is needed—what actors call a 'beat'—before her answer. In that beat the audience is given time to transfer its attention from one girl to the other.

'How *could* it *be*' is not only an expression of despair: it is also a half humorous half sad criticism of Liouba Ranevsky. The fatalism in her eyes is reflected in Anya's: so, another 'beat' takes the point of attention back to Anya. What follows happens the same way, as the point of attention darts back and forth between them like the ball in a tennis match. Then Lopahin enters at the opposite end of the room. The point of attention then has to sweep in an arc from one side of the stage to the other. Lopahin's joke is so extraordinary and unexpected that if the actor does not time it carefully it will be over before the audience can be made to realize that it has happened at all. But fortunately his actual entrance distracts the audience's eyes away from them to him. Another 'beat' before his joke—for if the audience cannot fully react to two effects at a time they certainly cannot savour the strange noise he makes should the 'Moo!' coincide with the movement of his entrance.

But after the joke the audience's eyes must come back to Varya. What is funny to him is far from funny to her, and the effect of Lopahin on her must not be missed. She must draw the attention away from him and back to her by some small movement, such as a turn of the head, before she speaks her line. Similarly the concern in Anya's voice and face, a deeper concern, possibly, than she has shown before, needs to be noted. So, she embraces Varya first, to bring the point of attention to herself, and speaks the line afterwards.

The power of movement to draw the eye will be noted: the converse is true; where the eye has too much to see the ear cannot listen. (The implication of this is to be met in every department of theatre, and particularly, of course, in the realm of the stage designer.)

We have seen now that the director in fact reverses the role of the hypnotist. In doing this his main preoccupations are twofold, to overcome the inertia of the audience, and to convey meaning with complete clarity. To achieve the former, and to continue to achieve it, he must avoid sameness throughout the entire span of the performance: at rehearsal he is on constant watch against it creeping in under his guard. He must listen acutely to the voices of his actors, and be ready to pounce on each sign of monotony of pace, pitch or volume. He must be sensitive to the vocal habits of each member of the cast in order to avoid the danger of repetitive rhythms. And of course he extirpates ruthlessly any repetitive writing in the script. In short, he works positively and in every possible way to provide *dramatic contrast* for the ear and for the eye. And to achieve *clarity of communication* he uses his means—the *theatrical elements* of pace, pitch, volume, suspense and physical action—in a manner which is conditioned by the basic needs of the audience.

In this a marked duality emerges. *Everything that the theatre artist does demands a careful balance between opposites.* The theatrical elements have been defined as necessary ways to excite, to hold, and to convey significance to an audience. They express, in fact, the *power* which directors and actors hold over the audience. But they are *also*, when looked at another way, a major part of the significance itself. The pauses and movements in the excerpt from *The Cherry Orchard* are part of the way in which an interpreter could make the audience aware of what is going on. But they also *are* what is going on, just as much as the words themselves. If pauses and movements and changes of pitch and so on are not used to convey meaning, but are used only because of the power inherent in them, the result is falseness and, in the perorative sense, 'theatricality'. The director, and, to a much larger extent the actor (for whom temptation is never absent) have always a choice before them. To be effective, merely, or to be true. (The right balance, of course, is to be effective *and* true.) The audience can very easily be played upon as an unsuspecting victim of the performer's self-indulgence. It was Sacha Guitry who described the actor as one who makes love to a thousand people every night. If the actor is successful at this love-making and the public yield to his blandishments while abandoning their judgment of what is truly sincere— then he is indeed as the king of beasts in the jungle. It is a question of taste. The unscrupulous seducer of the audience has said goodbye to taste, and in doing so has said goodbye also to all the preciseness of intention for which the author has striven. Coquelin's credo—and that of all interpretative artists who have not lost their sense of proportion—should be remembered: '*the duty of the actor is to respect his text: in whatever manner he delivers it he must speak what the author has written, nothing more, nothing less*'. The same goes for what happens between the lines as for the way the lines themselves are treated. The actor can, if he wishes, impose a rhythmic pattern on the words which has only a slender connection with their meaning, and still give the audience the stimulus it needs. If the director shows a reluctance to stimulate the audience by the right means (the use of all the dramatic contrasts in relation to the text) the performer is likely to try to save the situation by using the wrong means. The result will be a performance which is meretricious, yet, at least vital.

But now we should consider what performance actually is.

III · The Means

THE TOTALITY OF PERFORMANCE embraces the sympathetic interpretation of a play by director, actors, designer and all who have co-operated to bring it to life. This involves, as we have seen, far more than merely translating the script into audible and visible existence. It means a positive extension of an author's conception from the printed page into a new 'world', where all kinds of theatrical elements exist in a limbo, waiting for the imagination of the director to seize upon them and put them into a pattern. We can make a musical analogy here again: a wealth of notes exist in the musician's universe, and he chooses those that he wants and puts them in a harmonic / contrapuntal / rhythmic relationship, adding to them the elements of tone colour made possible by his choice of instrument, and adding, too, what he needs from the whole range of dynamics from *pianissimo* to *fortissimo*. The notes, their combinations and harmonies etcetera, the rhythms and dynamics, are the musical elements which the composer envisages and which the conductor will express. It is the same with the theatre director: *theatrical elements* exist for him to use, and these are the values or units out of which the pattern of performance is built.

We have seen in Chapter I that much can 'happen' in a pause. We have seen, too, how it can affect the audience. The dramatic pause, marked in directors' scripts and in prompt copies by the musical symbol '⌒', is in fact, the commonest tool of performance, the stock-in-trade of all actors, the most hard-worked of all the theatrical elements to be juggled with by the director. The reason is obvious—it is so very useful.

It can be a mere punctuation mark, separating one thought from another, or one scene from another. Alternatively, it can contain a world of significance. It can be extremely short, hardly more than the slightest of hesitations, or as long as the actor and the director think it will hold—fifteen or twenty seconds, which is long in stage time. It is the script which must determine how it is used. What fills the pause is the significance which an imaginative director, and an imaginative performer can find in the writing, nothing less and nothing more. The actor who uses the pause merely to demonstrate his power on the audience throws away his honesty.

In the three lines from *Hedda Gabler* already quoted Brack's 'I beg your pardon' comes after the briefest of hesitations— scarcely more than a breath, to indicate his surprise at Hedda's 'vine leaves' line. (If Hedda is being played by a star it is quite likely that the lady will want her Brack not to hesitate at all. Stars tend to dislike pauses made by the people they are playing with: they feel that as they will be making plenty of pauses on their own account, the scene will be slow if they encourage others to pause as well.) A minimal pause would, however, be right here—no more than what would naturally spring from a reminder to the actor to think before he speaks. Hedda has just said something odd and incomprehensible. Ibsen would not have put a question into Brack's mouth at this point if he were not intended to *show* bewilderment. He cannot show bewilderment unless there is an appropriate space in time for him to show it in.*

The length of a dramatic pause varies according to the importance of the work it does. The more complex the significance that is to be poured into it, the greater the space in time it will need to occupy.

What follows after Brack's question, and before Hedda replies 'Nothing', can be supercharged with significance. Many things surge through her consciousness at this moment of climax. The audience cannot take them in all together in

* See 'placing', pages 48, 49.

a lump: the actress has to present them in natural sequence, yet using her art and technique to express each element of the pause with clarity. Hedda has first to shake herself out of her reverie about Eilert Lovborg. There is much for her to think about, since Brack has just told her of Eilert's debauch at Madame Diana's—a relapse not quite of Hedda's intending. The news disturbs her. When Brack's question comes, it falls, first, on deaf ears. Hedda is absorbed by the image of Eilert 'with vine leaves in his hair' and tortured by the contrast between it and the truth. For the first time, her confidence is shaken. An actress capable of playing Hedda can make a great deal of this, and she cannot convey it in a mere flash. But now Brack's voice, in a delayed reaction, bores through the reverie, and she hears at last that he has not understood what she said in her previous line. (How could he have done, how could his narrow bourgeois mind, however sharp, have understood her high-flown fancying? Her words were not intended for him anyway.) Brack's question is not worthy of an apology for not replying to it within a reasonable time: indeed, it is scarcely worth an answer at all. Hedda's expression changes. In her own good time, she shows that she has heard him. She can afford to keep him waiting: she has the power that every beautiful woman possesses over a man who is attracted by her, but for whom she does not care a straw (she does not realize yet that the tables have been turned and that now it is Brack who possesses power over her). She slowly turns her head towards him, for, of course, it was averted for the vine leaves' line. She looks at him, aware of her power and still able sub-consciously to enjoy it. And finally she brushes off his question with a contemptuous answer.*

This particular pause, then, can contain at least half-a-dozen elements (others can no doubt be found: this move-

---

* This sequence of events occurred when Sián Phillips played *Hedda Gabler* at the Nye Theater, Oslo, and subsequently at the Vanbrugh Theatre. The translator's lines were slightly amended.

ment of the play is wide open to imaginative interpretation).
Each element has to convey its message clearly: each has to
have *outline*, that is a beginning, a duration, and an end,
(otherwise the effect will seem blurred and muddled). But all
the elements must also be bound together by the sense of
momentum of the actors and director: they need to be
enclosed within the totality of this moment of silent acting.

The moment, be it noted, is another example of the duality
of theatre. It contains a warning, and the better the actress,
the more necessary the warning. There is danger here that
exhibition may outweigh *communication*: that the beauty
of the actress, her power of personality, her grace of movement, and her power over the audience, can all of them seem
more important than what is happening inside Hedda. All
these qualities are qualities that belong to Hedda. Three, at
least, out of four of them should be among any actress's assets,
and her assets are there to be used, particularly her power to
compel attention. Without this no audience will be disposed
to watch her at all. It is therefore a matter of the finest judgment to determine just where Hedda's turn of the head, if
more than a certain emphasis is placed upon it, ceases to
contribute to her performance and becomes a distraction.
Judged rightly it can be a moment of theatre magic. Judged
wrongly it is no more than vulgarity. Only the director,
watching rehearsals develop from his objective position, can
control such a moment.

There are many other uses of the dramatic pause. One
of them is for 'pointing' (that is for bringing into appropriate
prominence) a line that needs to stand out from among others.
Consider Millament, ready at last to capitulate to Mirabell:

These articles subscribed, if I continue to endure you
a little longer, I may by degrees dwindle into a wife.

The phrase '. . . dwindle into a wife' is the sort of line which
should provoke laughter but will fail to do so if it is not
prepared for. The comedic content consists solely in connect-

B*

ing 'dwindle' with 'wife': * the actress prepares the audience
for the joke by an infinitesimal hesitation before 'dwindle'.
The justification for this in terms of truth is that Millament
needs a fraction of a second for her nimble brain to survey
the choice of intransitive verbs and to alight upon the
appropriate one. The justification in terms of the audience is
that this moment, breaking the rhythmic flow which precedes
it, tells them that the joke is coming. The pause actually
creates a moment of suspense, during which and because of
which, the audience concentrates, waiting for something to
happen. The old time music hall comic had a prescription for
the clarity of effect needed to get laughs: 'tell 'em you're
going to do it; do it; then tell 'em you've done it'. Pointing is
a subtle refinement of the first part of this process. (The more
delicate the writing, the more subtle, naturally, the interpretation. It is noteworthy, however, how much of the subtlest
techniques in acting have grown from the broad methods of
the past: the difference is of degree, not of kind.) It is the
tension of suspense, a vital need of the audience, which makes
this pause necessary before the joke, in order to make it work.
All pauses that come before the line or before the important
theatrical statement (be it comedic, or emotional or intellectual) are suspense pauses. The more powerful the statement
the longer the preceding pause needs to be. The Hedda pause
before her 'nothing' would have to be short indeed, since the
reply is so brief a negative, unless some such sequence of
thought and movement as described were done. But the pause
before, say, Beatrice's 'Kill Claudio', in Much Ado About
Nothing would clearly be a long one since the anticipation
here is high and the answer a bombshell.

The last part of the old rule—'tell 'em you've done it'—is
achieved by a pause; but this one follows the effect. When a
line of importance has been said the audience needs time to
take it in. The process of mental digestion must be allowed to
happen. If the line is comedic, moreover, the moment extends

* See Chapter V on Comedy.

itself while the audience laugh. If the laughter is not antici-
pated in this way, the audience will not realize they are
meant to laugh and will not do so. But both subtlety and
good judgment are essential here: the performer does not
obviously wait for the laugh. It is a matter rather of letting
the thought continue after the line is spoken: the words finish,
but their impact carries on. '. . . and dwindle into a wife'
needs to be savoured and enjoyed. It is as when a bell is
struck; the clapper has done its work but the reverberation
continues.*

An interesting example of this is the final curtain of
Tchehov's Ivanov. Tchehov was 26 when he completed this
play, and still inexperienced in craftsmanship. He ends his
last Act as follows:

> IVANOV: Leave me alone!
> *(Steps aside and shoots himself.)*

The events which lead up to the curtain have been fast
moving, at times verging on the farcical. The audience has
not been prepared by the author for tragedy, and, of course,
to the many other characters who fill the stage at Sasha's
wedding party the event is totally unexpected. The problem
of when to bring down the curtain is considerable. It cannot
come down immediately upon the pistol shot, for Ivanov's
sudden death is a tremendous and terrible moment: an
immediate curtain will cut this moment off as ruthlessly as
the switching off of a symphony on the radio before the final
chord has died away. Yet if there is to be the long reverberative pause, what happens to the other characters? Tchehov
has given them nothing to say or do. What is required is a
device to allow the curtain to fall slowly at least four or five
seconds after the pistol shot, while also justifying complete
stillness on the stage. A successful device is to use music. A

---

* The famous dramatic coach and voice teacher Bertie Scott called
this the *follow-through*, likening it to the successful conclusion of a
professionally perfect stroke in golf. It is a good simile.

fraction of a second after the shot the musicians strike up a triumphant tune. All on the stage are frozen into immobility first by the shock of the event, and secondly by the irony and incongruity of the music. Just as they begin to come out of their trance and as Doctor Lvov and a servant begin to move towards the body, the curtain comes slowly down.*

This is the principle of the 'follow-through' extended beyond the field of individual actor to that of the timing of the production itself. Without the 'follow-through' this curtain is as dead to the senses as a bell muffled with felt.

At the other end of the scale is the really strong effect, demanding the really 'long' pause. When Othello strangles Desdemona, and she appears to be dead, it is, comparatively, a long pause indeed before the knocking off stage should start and Emilia's voice be heard. The emotional climax to which Othello builds is tremendous. When the murder is actually performed the moment of tragedy is so powerful that it must be given its due suspension in time. In this way it is clothed in appropriate importance, and the audience given its chance of mentally digesting the horror of the act. Moreover, if Othello is acting properly the audience will need time to get over its shock, and to begin to wonder what will be happening next. While it is still in its shocked state it *isn't interested* in what is to follow.

This brings us to yet another attribute of the dramatic pause: its use as a *separator* of different theatrical qualities, moods and ideas. For example, let us take a moment in the scene between Trigorin and Nina in Act II of *The Seagull*. Trigorin, at some length, has been telling Nina of the trials of a writer. As he talks to her about himself he becomes conscious of her attractions, and in realizing these he is unable to resist giving a powerful sexual overtone to his own words: this has its effect on her. There is a turning point in the scene where each of them becomes conscious, for the first time,

* This is what happened in the production of *Ivanov* at the Arts Theatre in 1950, and at the Vanbrugh Theatre in 1965.

of the physical magnetism of the other and of feelings which
have nothing at all to do with the literary subject of their
conversation.

TRIGORIN: . . . And so it will be till I die—just charming
    and clever, charming and clever, and never anything
    more: and when I'm dead, and my friends stroll past
    my grave, they'll say 'Here lies Trigorin—a very fine
    writer, but not so good as Turgenev'.

NINA: You must forgive me, but really I refuse to accept
    all that. You are simply spoilt by success.

On the face of it Nina's comment, following naturally on
what Trigorin has said, is no more than the scoring of a
minor point in conversationship. That is all the lines actually
say in so many words. But director and actors, of course,
must delve more deeply. Given the natures of the two
characters, given Nina's 'This is a dream!' which finishes the
Act soon after Trigorin exits, and given what happens to
Nina afterwards, it is clear enough that much has to occur
between the lines in this scene. This 'much' is the crescendo
of unstated but clearly powerful sexual desire. After Trigorin's
'not so good as Turgenev' there is a kind of finality, as there
is about any epitaph: this argues the need for a pause in any
case, as a dramatic punctuation mark. But the moment
demands rather more. After this point—the earliest possible
point in the scene, if the scene is carefully examined—Nina
feels for the first time in her life the existence of something
stronger than herself. Here is her moment of realization of
dark impulses far removed from the polite pretences of genteel
society. It is here that she loses her innocence, not, later, in
the Slavyansky Bazaar.

The pause needed before she speaks is therefore very long
indeed, in the theatrical scale. It has to separate the ideas to
which she has been listening—Trigorin's thoughts about his
profession and so forth—from the new ideas which spring

from his physical proximity and from the telepathy of his physical instincts. The audience needs time for digestion of the first. Nina needs time for realization (not with her mind, though with her senses) of the second. And the audience, again, needs time to adjust itself to the change of level at which the drama is being carried. (With perceptive acting and direction they will of course have been aware of the two levels all the time : they will be wiser than the characters themselves. At this point, they and Nina must be together in their feeling that something of enormous importance has happened to her.)

The suspense-tension of the audience makes the moment also tremendously emphatic. As Nina's feelings emerge from her expressive silence the audience is wondering what she is going to say when she finally speaks. Is she going to say something which will lead to their emotions becoming specific? Or is she going to attempt to conceal that she has been affected in this alarming way? As they speculate on the outcome of the pause the audience's apprehensions are sharpened. Nina chooses the second course. She makes her minor conversational point, but the words are simply a cover for her true feelings, which from now on are clearly seen to be behind everything she says or does. From now on, as a result of the revelation which the pause has made possible, the audience watches Nina with the most concentrated attention.

There are other kinds of dramatic pause—the pause that springs from thought or motive (the Hedda pause with Judge Brack is also one of these, for she deliberately ignores his question, partly with the intention of snubbing him). And there can be the pause which springs only from characterization. When Arkadina in *The Seagull* has that terrible scene with her son after bandaging his head in Act III she deliberately tries to hurt him, for he has made an uncomplimentary comment on Trigorin, her lover. And Konstantin doesn't care what he says to her; jealous of Trigorin, he resents his mother having anything to do with him :

ARKADINA: ... you're not fit to write so much as a tenth-rate revue. You are a paltry Kiev tradesman—a hanger on!

KONSTANTIN: Money grubber!

ARKADINA: Guttersnipe!

    (*Konstantin sits down and sobs quietly.*)

Nonentity!

    (*She walks restlessly up and down.*)

Don't cry. You mustn't cry. You mustn't. . . .

    (*She weeps, kissing him on the forehead.*)

My own little boy, forgive me. Forgive your wicked mother.

After 'Nonentity!', clearly, Arkadina needs a separating pause, marking the transition from her invective to her remorse: that much is obvious. But there is a subtler pause possible, *before* 'Nonentity!' Mother and son have worked up a venomous yet childish quarrel, which has swept them both along in its own rhythm. The invective on both sides is heedless and irresponsible, and each tries to cap the other in hurtful offensiveness. Then after 'Guttersnipe!' comes the stage direction: 'Konstantin sits down and sobs quietly'. Clearly his sensitivity outweighs his desire to hurt. Arkadina is not callous, only selfish: she loves her son in her own not very admirable way. It is inconceivable that she should be entirely unaffected by the spectacle of his collapse into tears. Yet she not only continues the quarrel but flings at Konstantin the most damaging, the most unforgivable epithet she could possibly have thought of: 'Nonentity!' Very soon after doing so she is quick in remorse and asks his forgiveness. The actors and the director may well ask themselves how she could use such a word to her own son, and then, so suddenly, perform a volte face into contrition: is she so insincere and so superficial as to be utterly blind to Konstantin's feelings? Tchehov did not create characters which are 'good' or 'bad', 'sensitive' or 'insensitive'. So what is the answer? The answer is a brief pause before 'Nonentity!' during which Arkadina, having just thought of the word which would most hurt Konstantin, realizes at the same time the enormity of using it. But the actress in her, together with the uncontrollable pleasure which she gets from dominating other people (and particularly her son), makes her shrink only for a second. She hesitates, with the word just about to form on her lips: then, fully knowledgeable of her cruelty, and, indeed, horror-struck by this vision of herself, she lets it out. With such ambivalence behind the venom her remorse and contrition are intensified, and 'forgive your wicked mother' means so much the more.

There is yet a further use of the pause—the 'placing' by its use of a particular line of effect, particularly where comedy is involved. The audience, it will be remembered, can focus fully only on one specific effect at a time (though it can enjoy a generalized 'harmonic' effect perfectly well). While some effects of comedy are prepared for, there are others whose aptness depends on the unexpectedness with which they are presented:

LEBEDYEV: France's politics are clear and definite. The French know what they're after. They want to skin the German sausages, and they want nothing more. But the Germans, my friend, it's a different tune altogether. The Germans have got quite a lot of fish to fry, besides France.

COUNT SHABELSKY: Nonsense!

A number of factors combine to make Shabelsky's comment a laugh line, but without the *particular* factor of the timing of 'Nonsense' the laugh will not happen—however careful the actors may be about the others.* This, it will be remembered, is the opening of *Ivanov's* third Act, by which time the

* See Chapter V on Comedy.

relationship of the two men—always ready to argue on small matters like schoolboys—should have been built up: factor number one. Second, both characters are pleasantly intoxicated, as a study of the scene and of the characters will clearly show (although Tchehov characteristically does not find it necessary to state the fact specifically). Third, Lebedyev's opening speech is ponderous and elaborate. He repeats himself, emphasizing the fact by making a feature of the full stops (themselves 'pauses', but short ones), and succeeds, with an air of making a pronunciamento, in saying nothing of the slightest importance. Fourth, there is an unexpected contrast between the lengthy elaboration of Lebedyev's line and the easy brusqueness of Shabelsky's answer to it. These elements will combine to achieve the audience's laughter, *but only if* the fifth factor is also present—a pause, 'long' in theatrical time, before 'Nonsense!'

The need for this pause springs partly from the audience's suspense-tension, and partly also from their limited ability to focus attention. Throughout Lebedyev's speech the audience is concentrating on him almost exclusively. It is taking pleasure in the discovery that he is enjoying someone else's drink in someone else's room, and it is generally sizing up the situation. Lebedyev now stops talking, and the actor playing him relapses into torpor: this is essential, for the attention of the audience must now be directed *away* from him and *towards* Shabelsky. The audience now look at Shabelsky. He is seen to be thinking, yet thinking in an abstracted way as is usual with those who have had rather too much to drink. Slowly on Shabelsky's face appears the expression of a man, under some difficulty, about to try to say something sagacious. But Shabelsky brings forth a mouse: all that comes is the school-boyish contradiction which indicates that in all the years of their intimate relationship nothing has changed: given the appropriate stimulus the Count will always behave in the way the audience has come to expect.

We have now examined some of the uses of the pause. We

have seen how it helps to convey thought and character; how it points comedy and emphasizes laugh lines; how it creates suspense, and how its reverberative value adds savour to a line; how as a separator of different ideas it actually makes possible the expression of ideas not in the script at all; and, finally, how it can direct the attention of the audience where actor and director want it to be.

But of course, we have examined the pause in isolation, and nothing that happens in the theatre is ever really isolated from anything else. Performance must never cease to *flow*: the pause is always a relative quantity. It is only one of the theatrical elements at the director's disposal, and must therefore be considered in relation to what follows.

The use of dynamics—the volume and type of articulation applied to words—is, of course, an important means of dramatic emphasis. It is also a means which is, insofar as volume is concerned, over-used, particularly by bad actors and amateurs, who tend to simplify its expression into extremes. Extremes have their value, certainly, when used appropriately. The thing to realize about them however is that unless they are used with great economy they quickly become monotonous. It is, of course, *variety* of volume which is essential: this means that it is the infinitely graduated range *between* extremes that have to be explored, in relation to the sense of the lines.

What can be far more interesting than variety in volume—and what is only rarely understood—is the importance of individuality of articulation. The dynamics of articulating a single word in relation to its context can have tremendous value. 'I *may by degrees dwindle into a wife*' depends for its effect on more than the comic spirit of the actress, and the pointing and isolation of the joke, with appropriately subtle pauses. It depends on how the word 'dwindle' is actually said. 'Dwindle' is the key word; no other word would do as well.

It needs emphasizing by the actress, otherwise its quality will not be sharp enough in focus for the audience to apprehend it. The initial pause has prepared for it (*tell 'em you're going to do it*), the reverberative pause after it has given them their moment of digestion (*tell 'em you've done it*). But what about 'Do it'? How can the word '*dwindle*' be underlined, yet in the subtlest of ways, as befits the subtlest English comedy of classic times? The word cannot be 'hit' with any kind of force without destroying the delicacy of the entire sentence. It can only be framed cunningly by a very slight difference of tempo in the articulation of the vowel of its first syllable. Thus the 'i' of 'dwindle' lasts fractionally longer than the vowels of the rest of the phrase. That is the technique of the matter: in terms of its truth, which must also be obeyed, what more natural than that Millament is herself rather fond of the word she has chosen, and that consequently she should dwell upon it, lovingly, for a second? When words matter, they matter indeed. By 'leaning on the words' in varying degrees of emphasis director and performer can obtain something very like the variety of tone available to an accomplished instrumentalist.

It follows that such nuances are not confined to single words. Variety of this kind can obviously be found in complete sentences, in whole speeches and in complete scenes. In these we are concerned with tempo and pace.

Tempo, which is variable, and used to differentiate different elements of a performance must be distinguished from Pace which applies generally to the complete production. (It is unfortunate that the terms are very frequently confused.) Here are a few lines from *Uncle Vanya*: Sonya is telling Yelena of her love for Astrov:

SONYA: . . . I couldn't restrain myself yesterday from telling Uncle Vanya that I love him [Astrov]. . . . And all the servants know that I love him. Everybody knows.

YELENA: Does he?

SONYA: No. He never notices me.

YELENA: (*meditatively*) He's a strange man. . . . Do you
think. . . ? Tell me, will you let me speak to him?
I'll be very careful—just a hint. . . . .

(*pause*)

Yes, that will be best, or who knows how long you
may go on in uncertainty. . . . Do let me!

The *pauses* here are clear enough—the shortest of breaths
before Sonya makes her admission with 'No', the dots and
commas and directions that Tchehov has indicated. But of the
tempo there is no indication, though in 'Meditatively' there is
a clue as to how Yelena should begin her lines. She is thinking, not mainly of what Sonya has said, for the girl's state
of mind has been apparent to her for some time. She is thinking, rather confusedly, about Astrov himself, her disturbing
attraction to him and its dangers, and wondering how the
knowledge that now Sonya knows that *she knows* is going to
affect the situation. Hence the *legato tempo* of 'He's a strange
man. . . .' Then she gets an idea—the exciting idea that she
can use this situation to contrive a tête-à-tête with Astrov:
'Do you think. . . ?' has a quicker tempo; behind it is eagerness
tempered with caution. 'Tell me, will you let me speak to
him?' is quicker still as Yelena's pulse beats a little faster.
Then comes her need to show concern for Sonya's feelings:
'I'll be very careful—just a hint' is slower, not only because
she tries to reassure the girl by an expression of measured good
sense, but because she is ever so slightly disingenuous, she is
'acting' a little for Sonya's benefit. 'Yes, that will be best, or
who knows how long you may go on in uncertainty' is still
slower: it is abstracted, and she is now thinking less of what
she is actually saying than of how she will deal with Astrov
when she is alone with him and of how interesting that conversation will be. With 'Do let me' she is back in the present,
she is quicker and persuasively forceful.

Variety of tempo, it is clear, springs entirely from the nature of the writing—from what the words mean and the significance behind them. The better the dramatist the more apparent is the connection between thought and feeling, on the one hand, and the technical necessity of keeping the audience interested by variety of method, on the other. The more the dramatist fails in evocativeness, the more the director and the actor have to invent justifications for the variety which they inject into their treatment of the material. This is testing to their creativeness, and they must think hard to find motives of which the author may never have thought but which are vital to a compelling performance.

The tempo of a production is not solely a matter of what happens within a long speech. Variety is needed throughout whole scenes, indeed throughout the entire performance. Each sentence and each phrase has its appropriate tempo, according to its nature. The varying of the interval between the giving of a cue by one performer and the taking of it up by another, is an important factor. It is easy to appreciate this in measured dialogue such as the verbal duel between Judge Brack and Hedda Gabler.* The use for it is less obvious in quick-moving scenes, but application merely follows commonsense. For example:

BORKIN: Sir, you are offensive! I challenge you to a duel!

LVOV: My dear Borkin, I should consider it degrading not only to fight with you but even to talk to you. And Ivanov can receive whatever satisfaction he likes.

SHABELSKY: Sir, I'll meet you myself!

SASHA: Why? Why d'you insult him, gentlemen, let him tell me: why?

LVOV: Alexandra Pavlovna I do not denounce him without proofs. I came here, as an honest man, to open your eyes, and I beg you to listen to me.

* See page 25.

SASHA: What can you say? That you are an honest man? The whole world knows it!

The momentum of the last scene of *Ivanov* is here getting faster and faster. Events are speeding Ivanov towards the inevitable finish (it is less than two minutes away) like a brakeless vehicle rushing downhill to destruction. Nothing that the characters say at this point is motivated by good sense or measured thought. The pace in general is quick, that is, the actors 'jump' on their cues and there is little or no interval between cues and following lines. However, variety is essential, so the director must vary the almost non-existent interval just the same. He can find three opportunities for doing this. 'I challenge you to a duel!' is an unexpected and astonishing statement for the assembled company to hear. The shock it creates needs a reverberative pause. 'Sir, I'll meet you myself!' is a comedic line, in view of Count Shabelsky's advancing years.* There is scarcely time at this stage in the play to give it full comedy treatment, for if it had this the all-important momentum would be lost (the experienced director will know how often he must sacrifice a valuable effect for the sake of the good of the whole). None the less the line is delightful in the context and its absurdity should not be lost: it is worth a fractional pause after it is said. During the pause Shabelsky looks surprised at his own temerity: Sasha assimilates the turn events have taken, does not jump on her cue, but uses the brief moment to give 'spring' to the indignation which is growing in her. The third variation is there for the same reason. Sasha's 'What can you say. . . ?' is in fact the beginning of a long and contemptuous condemnation of Dr Lvov. She is intelligent: her mind works, despite her fury, and it works quickly. In the fractional pause before she begins her speech she has already discovered what she is going to say. And she says it with far more attack than would be possible if that little pause were not there.

---

* See the 'disparity which is large enough'. Comedy, page 111.

Now the pace must be considered, for *pace* is what binds all the elements of performance together. Much has been said about pauses, and the virtues of slowness as well as quickness in the speaking of dialogue, but if there is no conception of pace, then 'slowness' (which it is essential to remember is a *relative* term) becomes a deadening and absolute fact. We use the word 'pause' because we lack a better one. But we must not think of it as in any sense a hiatus: there is no such thing as a pause in which nothing is 'happening'. In fact, as we have seen, a very great deal can be happening. The more 'happens', that is, the greater the *content*, the more the pause is lengthened to accommodate it. But unless the director has an instinct for appropriate rhythm, that 'length' can very easily be over-estimated, and disaster will result. The director, as always, must study the sense of the lines and be sure of what is going on inside the people of the play. Such processes in a character's mind as decision, appraisal, judgment, acceptance or non-acceptance, are 'electric' and instantaneous. An actor has only to think of them and they are there, needing only a fractionally extended moment to ensure clarity, and to give the audience time to assimilate what has been expressed. Emotions are slower quantities than these processes of the mind, mainly because they are seldom simple, but are compounded of a number of nuances of feeling, each of which has to be indicated. A pause of emotion therefore will be a longer kind of pause, but here again its length must be confined to the shortest time necessary to do its work and no more. (What actors call 'milking' the pauses not only fatally slows up the pace of the performance, but also distorts truth itself.) Pace is always quicker in dialogue where the sense is on the surface, as in the six lines from the last Act of *Ivanov*. It is slower where the characters' thoughts and feelings range away from what they actually say. In the beginning of *Ivanov's* third Act quoted on page 48 each of the characters has a purpose in waiting on Ivanov. Their expressed thoughts are spoken, their deeper thoughts, which do not emerge till later in the Act, are what affect the pace of the scene. Each time they speak they have to struggle upwards, out of the level of their several preoccupations, and through the layer of alcoholic fog which weighs on them. Hence the length of the pauses in this scene.

The pause can possess its own kind of magic, which is felt in its silence, and is sensed in the many indefinable moments in theatre when time can seem to stop. It creates overtones we can't hear, but we know they are there and their presence, unquotable, inexplicable, is what makes one performance unforgettable compared to another. In the last six minutes of *The Cherry Orchard* scarcely anything is said but a succession of platitudes, a brother embraces his sister, a half-hearted attempt at a proposal comes to nothing, the luggage is taken out, the carriage takes the family away, the old butler comes in muttering, the sound of departing horses' hooves mingles with the chop-chop of the axes on the cherry trees. In the timing of the pauses between these happenings the actors can seem to hold the intangible in their hands, and each moment can be made to create a richness of experience so deep that it cannot be forgotten.

Movement, of course, is essential to the variety and the life of a performance. Like the dramatic pause, it has its dangers. Just as some actors may often be tempted to wait too long, because through the pause they see an escape from the discipline of the lines: the lines 'hold them down', the pause gives them the chance to 'act', so they tend to walk about too much, to use too much facial expression and too much gesture for the same reason. It is bad to yield to this temptation if only because it entails making the same statement twice over. It is true to say that for every move that takes place in the course of a performance there must be a justification. Usually that justification is to be found in the needs of the character: sometimes, as in avowedly artificial plays (*e.g.* Goldoni) or in plays where characters are *openly* 'impersonated' by *actors* (Brecht) the justification may lie in the technical needs of the performer. Meaningless movement is always deplorable: we know how easy it is for the audience's attention to wander, and movement can have extremely distracting properties, since it is always easier to watch than to listen. Conversely it is also true that a *significant* movement tends to lose sharpness of focus if lines, and particularly any important lines, are spoken with it. The movement of performers must therefore be very carefully controlled. Here is duality again, since the discipline of selection and artifice has to be applied to something which must originate from the spontaneity of the character and which, in the finished product, must appear to be precisely that.

Stage movement is of two kinds. In the last Act of Ibsen's *A Doll's House* Helmer walks deliberately to the letter-box because he wants to clear it. The movement is a conscious one: it is also a most important one, since both the audience and Nora know what is in that letter-box and are apprehensive. Both the audience and Nora, therefore, are impelled to watch Helmer's move, which is highly dramatic and makes a specific theatrical statement. Director and actor would, by instinct, organize it in such a way that it obeys the rules of clarity and is uncluttered by the distraction of words. On the other hand, when, later in the Act, Helmer is disturbed by the knowledge of Dr Rank's impending death, and later still when he knows of Nora's deceit, Ibsen gives Helmer the direction 'walking up and down'. In both these cases speeches of some length are clearly intended to be spoken by the actor on the move. The movements in Helmer are *unconscious* ones: they are not in conflict with the lines; in fact they add to them, helping to colour the disturbed state of mind which is already being expressed by the words. They may accompany the words, therefore, without distracting from them since the audience is not being asked to take in simultaneously two statements which conflict with each other.

But even movements of mood and atmosphere need to be carefully organized:

LOPAHIN: Up to now, the only people in the country have been the gentry and the farmers, but now the summer visitors have started. All the towns, even the little ones, have their belt of summer bungalows. And there's no doubt at all that in the next twenty years the number of summer visitors will grow enormously. Now they just come to drink tea on the verandah, but once they've leased their own land, they might very well come and set up housekeeping here and then your cherry orchard would become a real gold mine and keep you in happiness and luxury.

GAYEV: (*indignantly*) Nonsense!

VARYA: Two telegrams have come for you, Mama dear. (*She takes a key and opens an old bookcase: the lock shoots back with a ringing sound*) Here they are.

LIOUBA: They're from Paris. (*tears them up without reading them*) I've finished with Paris—

GAYEV: Do you know, Liouba, how old that bookcase is? A week ago I happened to take out the bottom drawer. . . . .

Interesting points emerge from an examination of this. Lopahin, it will be remembered, has been trying for some minutes to get Liouba Ranevsky to concentrate on his practical proposition that her cherry orchard should be cut down and made into building lots. She has refused to take him seriously, and the conversation has drifted away into frivolities about eating frogs—and crocodiles—in Paris. So, when Lopahin tries to return to his point with the speech above (after the frivolities have caused him to move away in frustration) he *deliberately* and *consciously* steps into the scene again

and comes closer to Liouba than he was before. He does not
move and speak his opening lines 'Up to now' *etc.*, at the
same time, but starts his cross a second *before* he starts speaking. Thus he emphasizes his attitude of impatience, and also
draws the attention of Liouba and the assembled company,
and the audience, to himself. Because the move is valuable,
it is kept sharply focussed, and free from distraction by
words: when he starts speaking the point of the words is also
sharpened by the quality of feeling expressed by the movement. He completes his speech. It makes out a good case—by
his standards—for Liouba to sell her orchard: the audience
is not unimpressed by what he has said. But Gayev is not in
the least impressed. His indignant 'Nonsense!', if properly
timed, will get a laugh. It will get a laugh, that is to say
provided Tchehov's stage direction is not slavishly followed.
(The stage directions of experienced authors are not intended
to be literally obeyed: such authors are only too aware of the
need for flexibility in these matters.) The stage direction says
here 'Enter *Varya* and *Yasha*'. If a director were actually to
let them come on at this particular point the result would be
a halt in the smooth flow of the scene: the double entrance,
if it came quickly on the cue of 'Nonsense!' would abruptly
cut off the reverberation of the line, destroy its placing, and
extinguish the laugh with complete finality. On the other
hand if the entrance were delayed enough to give 'Nonsense!'
its due moment, the scene would be harmfully slowed up:
the seconds taken up by Varya coming on, and then afterwards speaking (she cannot do both simultaneously: her
unexpected entrance would distract from what she has to
say) are so many seconds of deadness in which nothing is
happening.

Tchehov's stage directions cannot, therefore, be acted upon.
Yasha can come in very much later (for he is not needed yet).
And Varya will have to come in earlier, in fact, while Lopahin
is speaking. She must time the entrance carefully, remember-
ing the distracting powers of movement: if the entrance,

however, coincides *approximately*** with one of Lopahin's brief pauses for thought (that is at one of his fullstops in the text) the entrance, far from being a distraction, assumes a quality of counterpoint. Varya therefore comes in unobtrusively and *listens* quietly to the words of a man in whom she is very interested—whom indeed she might one day marry if asked. Because of her feelings for Lopahin, Gayev's 'Nonsense!' irritates her, and she looks at him with annoyance during the reverberative pause. Then to hide her irritation (for with her religious leanings she is well aware of the sinfulness of anger) she flings away *upstage* to where the bookcase is: face to face with the bookcase she is reminded by it of the telegrams (otherwise why should she have thought of it at that particular moment?), unlocks the drawer, and brings them down to Liouba. Note that these two movements are of different kinds (the first is a reflex action of distaste, the second a practical move to hand over the telegrams, coloured with Varya's disapproval of Liouba). But both make theatrical statements which cannot be made at this point in any other way. They are worth, therefore, the emphasis of isolation. She hands the telegrams to her stepmother as she says 'Here you are' and turns away. Liouba next has her moment of memory as she tears them up. It is an important moment for the actress playing her: the audience must be able to see in Liouba's eyes not only how much this lover in Paris has meant to her, but also how in any matter of significant love she would be out of her depth. Liouba must have the point of attention, and everyone else must be still. As soon as this special moment of Liouba's is over Gayev starts his famous speech about the bookcase. The actor will certainly want a reason for starting to rhapsodize about the bookcase at this particular point: the answer is that his readiness for romantic expatiation can be triggered off by all sorts of things. In this case it is a feeling of embarrassment at having Liouba's unseemly goings on in Paris brought up so abruptly. The actor will also want to

* See page 122 in regard to precision in comedy.

'enjoy' his bookcase speech, as Gayev certainly enjoys it, and is likely to oppose any suggestion such as follows here, on the ostensibly reasonable grounds that the bookcase speech is one of Gayev's 'moments' and that nothing should obtrude upon it. According to the rules of clarity which have so far emerged the actor would be right. Yet, imagine the following:

Gayev starts the bookcase speech. He has already established himself as sentimental, a little foolish, set in a pattern, not of thinking about life, but of reacting predictably to it. To those who know him there is no surprise in the bookcase speech: once he has started it everybody can predict the lines on which it will continue. For everyone on the stage therefore the speech has no interest whatsoever, and there is no reason why they should listen to it at all. For the audience, however, there is of course a great deal of interest in the speech not because it adds up to a statement about anything at all, but because it is a part, like the imaginary billiard cues, the sweets and the comfortable self-deception, of the mosaic of Gayev's character. Here, it might seem, the duality of the theatre poses an insoluble problem—the needs of the audience for a sharply focused and clear-cut source of communication, and the needs of the characters to behave as in fact they must behave if they are to be true to themselves, cannot apparently be reconciled. Yet it is unthinkable that the truth should be sacrificed to any 'rule' about clarity or the needs of the audience: the reconciliation must be made. On carefully examining the bookcase speech, however, the problem disappears. The speech, like so much in Tchehov, is not specific: what matters in it is its flavour and its general character. As soon as the audience has appreciated this (which it can quickly do since it takes its cue from the inattention of the other characters), it needs to concentrate upon it no more than they do. It is free to let its thoughts wander at will—just as they do. It does not *need*, therefore, to concentrate solely on Gayev: after his words in the second half of the speech, 'dear and most honourable bookcase', it can take in the whole picture, rather than a particular part of it. It can savour Pistchic, alternating between a desire to drop off into a doze and an eagerness to press for a loan; it can note what a special place in the family is held by Firs, as he sits down by his serving table in a corner. Most important of all it can note the strange equivocal relationship of Lopahin and Varya (which is not even suggested in the text until Act II but the existence of which can usefully be hinted at here) provided two almost simultaneous movements are made.* After Gayev has addressed the bookcase in the words quoted above, Lopahin moves, not suddenly, but slowly and *in the same rhythm as Gayev's* speech, to put his coffee cup on the table behind the sofa. Immediately Varya also moves to the same table to pour him out a second cup. A look of understanding passes between them. The cup is poured, and both return to their places. By this slow, sweeping movement of these two characters, the eye of the audience is led in turn to look at the others, and to take in the whole stage picture. There is a trance-like quality about the movement: temporarily Varya and Lopahin—and everybody else—are, in a way, hypnotized by the inevitability and familiarity of Gayev's foolish and endearing lines. To use the ever-helpful musical analogy, this is a kind of counterpoint, pleasing for its own sake, while the whole sequence of events constitutes a 'moment' which serves to crystallize the essence of each character in the audience's mind.

Movement, then (like the other theatrical elements that are available to the director), is not only a means to variety and so to stimulation of the audience. It is a positive contributor to the expression of character, feeling, thought and atmosphere. It also exemplifies the duality of theatre in another way, since it is the only means whereby the stage picture itself can be formed, and changed, in relation to the development of the performance with its differing moods and situations.

* See plan of setting on page 67, Fig. 5.

Décor and grouping have to be considered together—the former coming first, since the masses, levels and angles of the setting affect the way the characters must sort themselves out upon it. The principles involved stand on the logic of composition to be observed in any art gallery. But there is also a logic of theatrical commonsense which should be easy to perceive. Let us examine the setting for *The Cherry Orchard*, Act I, on page 67 and the thinking which leads to its being shaped the way it is.

Tchehov requires three doors, a window, the bookcase (prominent), sufficient chairs and tables for convenience of the characters, and a Russian stove. *Three* doors in an ordinary room are somewhat unusual. The Tchehovian scenic convention is a naturalistic one: although this has been broken in recent years in a number of productions which have deliberately avoided naturalism, yet there is always the strongest of aesthetic arguments for presenting naturalistic theatre in the kind of setting for which the author wrote: reasonable plausibility should therefore be aimed at, so that the number of doors is not so obvious. This argues that only one of them should face the audience while the other two should be set in the side walls where they perform their function without constantly reminding the audience of their existence. The principal door is the door from the nursery to the courtyard of the house. Its importance lies not in the fact that more entrances and exits are made from it than from any of the others, but in the fact that the general entrance of the main characters at the beginning and their exit at the end 'frame' the play and provide what may well be thought the two most memorable moments in it. The door can evoke the necessary feelings of expectancy and finality only if it stares the audience in the face: this is the one, then, which is placed in the back wall. The entrance of Liouba, Gayev, Pistchic, Varya, Anya and Carlotta with her dog is quite a procession. For its full effect we must be able to see them all on the stage together as they cross: they must therefore travel some distance in view of the audience. This means that this door must not be in the centre of the back wall but some distance away from it. So we get this:

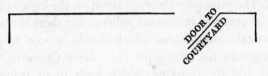

Fig. 1   **AUDIENCE**

Now where should the other doors be located, *upstage* or *down stage* in the side walls? There are disadvantages to the latter position: the thoroughfare to the door must be clear of furniture for smooth movement to and from it. If a door is placed *down stage* the thoroughfare must also be *down stage* and all furniture kept clear of it and above it.

This would automatically move the action *upstage* and lessen the contact of the actors with the audience.* So at least one of the other doors should be *upstage*:

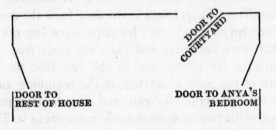

Fig. 2   **AUDIENCE**

* See pages 72 and 163, acting areas.

But before these doors are irrevocably set opposite each
other, as above, the whereabouts of the window must be
settled. The window is even more important than the doors,
for through it must be seen the cherry orchard, the *leitmotiv*
of the play, from which its whole atmosphere is born. Should
not the window be set in the back wall, dominating the
production, and providing a vista of cherry trees which
everybody in the theatre will be able to see? This is precisely
where, in many productions of the play, the window is
situated :

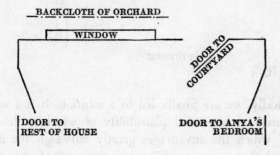

Fig. 3

There are various objections to this arrangement. It is
unlikely, architecturally. It forces those characters who need
to act in reference to the window far *upstage*, where they are
separated from the audience and inevitably masked by furniture. Worst of all it will force Liouba and Gayev either to act
with their backs to the audience when Liouba has her long
speech about the cherry orchard, or to 'cheat' their faces away
from the window so that their faces can be seen. Assuredly,
then the window must be set in one of the side walls, so that
the characters can stand before them looking out and being
seen by the audience in something rather better than profile.

c

But this, whether it is placed above or below one of the doors makes architectural nonsense:

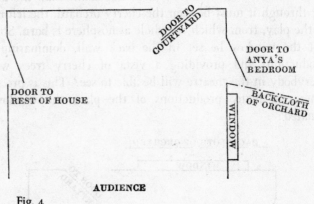

Fig. 4

Logically, we are finally led to a solution. It is a solution the purely architectural plausibility of which is debatable, but of which the advantages greatly outweigh the defects. (So much that is seen on the stage is the result of an inevitable compromise of apparent irreconcilables: this matters not in the least, if the resulting evocation is powerful enough to affect the audience as actor, director, and designer wish.) The advantages of Fig. 5 are:

1. Both principal door and window are dominating features.
2. The double window is not masked by furniture and audience see cherry orchard clearly.
3. Liouba and Gayev can act to the cherry orchard without turning their backs on the audience.
4. Window seat placed above *down stage* door to Anya's room provides a natural venue for the Varya–Anya scene, distinguishing this scene 'geographically' from others.
5. Furniture disposes itself naturally on this floor plan, giving clear thoroughfares to exits.

(The plans are for demonstration only and are not to scale.)

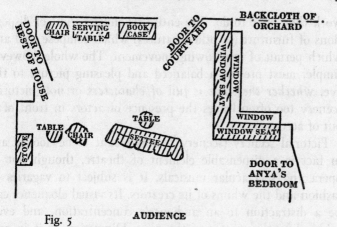

Fig. 5   AUDIENCE

We have, of course, been considering an old-fashioned type of setting for a play of an era which is no longer with us. Modern attitudes to scenery can free directors and designers from the shackles of realism. When a door or a window is indicated merely by an open frame in front of a surround of black curtains—or the brick walls of the theatre itself—we are spared such a problem as how to avoid Anya's going into a bedroom which, logically speaking, cannot be where we have put it. But, if architectural considerations are less frequent today (though there will always be plays which need the solidity of three walls and a 'fourth')* other factors remain to be reckoned with. The set must create the appropriate atmosphere, without overwhelming the actors, as often happens where a fashionable designer is allowed his head by a weak director, or where a director who fancies himself as a designer indulges himself with his own stage pictures. The entrances must be conveniently positioned in regard to the

* Most plays written for the naturalistic theatre need naturalistic settings. This is particularly true of the plays of Ibsen and Tchehov where the audience needs often to be aware of the forces of nature outside the 'fortress' of solid walls. Where conditions preclude naturalism, as in the Chichester Theatre, the audience still like to *imagine* a naturalistic relationship of walls and windows, even though they cannot see this.

work they have to do. The entire set must permit of disposi-
tions of furniture (or other features) which compose well and
which permit of free-flowing movement. The whole, however
simple, must present a balanced and pleasing picture to the
eye, *whether the stage is full of characters or not* (pictorial
scenery too often leaves the presence of actors in front of it
out of account).

Pictorial scenery (scenery that is *meant* to be 'looked at')
in fact is a dispensable element of theatre, though not of
opera and spectacular musicals. It is subject to vagaries of
fashion and the whims of its creators. Its visual eloquence can
be a distraction to an audience's concentration, and even
inimical to the matter of the play. Discussion of it in any
detail is not properly within the scope of a book about the
director in the theatre. Where it has to be used it is the
designer who must give the director what he wants—and
not the other way round. The *kind* of setting used, however,
depends not only upon the kind of play but upon the type
of theatre in which the play is to be acted. Grouping, which
is so intimately dependent on the setting, can only be examined in relation to the proscenium arch and the modern
divergencies from the picture-frame stage which have grown
out of it.

Proscenium theatre suffers today from an aura of obsolesc-
ence, which is curious not only because to relegate it to the
scrap heap would entail the extinction of ninety-nine per cent
of our theatres, but also because it remains, at least in modified
form, more adaptable to different kinds of drama than any
other species. Proscenium theatre (as well as the straight-
fronted open-stage theatre, which is 'picture-frame theatre
without the frame') still dominates our ideas about stage
grouping; so much so that difficulties are encountered when
we diverge from it, as we shall see later.

The practicalities of grouping, of course, have their roots
in the actor, and the actor's need to deploy his powers of
expression in the most effective way. The actor is at his most

effective only when *both his eyes,* and therefore most of his
features, are visible to the audience. (The truth of the corollary
that his voice, although his primary instrument, approaches
inaudibility the more he turns *upstage* or the less the illumination upon him, is demonstrated in the theatre every day.)
Thus, in the proscenium theatre, the dominating positions for
the actor have traditionally been variants of the following
basic floor plans, where A is the leading man (not to scale):

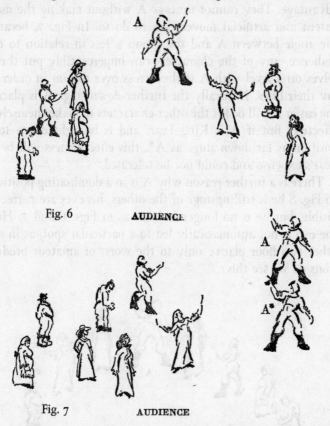

Fig. 6   AUDIENCE

Fig. 7   AUDIENCE

In both these positions A can address the others in such a
way that both his eyes can be seen: his gain in effectiveness,
because of this, is increased by a corresponding loss in effec-

tiveness by the subordinates who, when they speak to him, will only be in profile, and whose eyes may well be invisible altogether to some members of the audience. (However *King Lear* is staged, the king himself in the opening scene will be found in one or other of these positions, since otherwise he cannot possibly dominate his court.) Note that Fig. 7 is, however, more democratic, less rigid, than Fig. 6, where the lesser characters, when they have to speak are fixed in their disadvantage. They cannot *upstage* A without making the most patent and artificial movements to do so. In Fig. 7, because the angle between A and the group is less in relation to the audience, any of the characters can imperceptibly put themselves on a level with A if they cross over to him in order to say their lines. Naturally the further *down stage* A is placed, the easier it will be for the other characters to make themselves effective. But if A is King Lear, and is brought down to a position as far *down stage* as A*, this effectiveness will be at Lear's expense and could not be tolerated.

There is a further reason why A is in a dominating position. In Fig. 8 he is still *upstage* of the others, his eyes are perfectly visible, but he is no longer *isolated* as in Figs. 6 and 7. Here the eye is not automatically led to a particular spot, as in the other two floor plans: only in the worst of amateur productions do we see this:

Fig. 8   AUDIENCE

Isolation has, for good reason (when not abused) always been regarded as an essential means of emphasizing an actor who has a great deal to say or demands at any time to have the point of attention.

Fig. 9   **AUDIENCE**

In Fig. 9 A is just as important a figure as in Figs. 6 and 7, *provided* he is not required to turn *upstage* in order to speak to the group. Wherever *Hamlet* is staged on the face of the globe, he is likely to be found in some or even all of his soliloquies in something closely approximate to this position. A factor other than isolation is working here, and it is this factor, springing directly from the post-Ibsen/ Tchehov revolution, which has brought about the modern changes in theatre architecture.

In the heyday of the linear drama and the actor-manager 'projection' of voice was all important, as theatres became bigger and bigger with the introduction and improvement of stage lighting. Power, not subtlety, was what was needed, and thus the *upstage* positions for the dominating character as in Figs. 6 and 7, with their obvious advantages, assumed their traditional forcefulness. Before the Tchehovian water-shed it was not particularly noticed that there was at least one grave disadvantage, which the new subtler methods of acting quickly exposed. For *the further away an actor is from the audience the less effective he becomes.* There is a powerful force which flows from the very centre of an actor's being to the receptive *antennae* of the audience. This force has nothing to do with his voice, and it diminishes very rapidly the further *upstage* he goes. The bringing *down stage* of an entire group by even as little as a foot or two can increase the apparent vitality and vividness of the acting to quite an astonishing degree. The realization of this has led to those divergencies from the proscenium stage which are familiar to us today— the so-called 'open' stage,* the stage known in America as the 'thrust' stage,† and 'theatre-in-the-round'.‡ All these have sprung from a recognition of this mysterious current that flows from performer to audience and from a desire to bring the two closer together. The open stage atempts this by seeming to abolish that division between the two caused by the interposition of the proscenium. In fact it is not the proscenium and its curtain that create the barrier: proscenium theatres can be designed in which the barrier does not exist at all, *e.g.* the Yvonne Arnaud Theatre, Guildford, and the Playhouse, Nottingham. The barrier is merely a question of distance between the stage and the first row of the stalls: the abolishment of that nineteenth-century excrescence, the orchestra pit, together with purposeful design can reduce this to almost nothing. The thrust stage seeks to close the gap by bringing the actors apparently *among* the audience, while theatre-in-the-round triumphantly places the performers plumb in the middle of the crowd.

The real advantages, however, of 'open', 'thrust' and 'round' stages turn out not to be artistic as much as economic. It is far, far cheaper to build any of these than to build a conventional theatre of comparable size. Purposeful movement and meaningful grouping are, however, more difficult to achieve in the former than in the latter, though even in the latter the task is great enough. When we remember that the audience, with its thirst for variety, needs the stage

* e.g. the stages of the Mercury Theatre, London, and the Phoenix, Leicester.
† The Festival Theatre, Chichester.   ‡ The Victoria Theatre, Stoke.

picture to be alive and always changing, when we remember too that the changes can come about only by the logical need in the characters for a movement to be made (except in comparatively rare instances of deliberate artifice) and that it is necessary at all times that characters of more than minimal importance should always be seen to the best dramatic advantage—the difficulties of the director in manoeuvring the characters on the stage can be seen to be great indeed. A glance at Figs. 6, 7, 8 and 9 will show that it is only by extreme ingenuity that the director avoids (*a*) monotony, if he doesn't change his grouping often enough, (*b*) fussiness, if he changes it too frequently, (*c*) ridicule if, as is easy to do with a number of characters on the stage, all having a good deal to say, he lands up with the situation depicted in Fig. 8, (*d*) obscurity, caused by inaudibility and loss of focus, if he causes the bulk of his characters to irritate the audience by masking each other (which Figs. 6, 7 and 9 show to be an ever-present danger), and finally (*e*) implausibility, if he cannot find a good *theatrical* reason for every move that is made.

None of these pitfalls are lessened by use of the new unconventional stages, while yet another hazard is added—the distraction for the audience of being unable to avoid looking at itself at the other end of the line of sight.

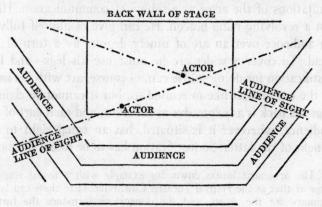

Fig. 10 Thrust stage

As a rule a raked auditorium limits what the audience sees of itself to the opposite front row. Also it is true, as the anti-proscenium enthusiasts vigorously point out, that the

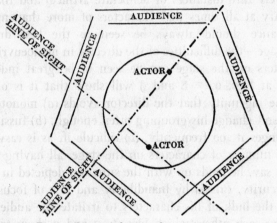

Fig. 11 Stage-in-the-round

spectator can be so absorbed by the reality of the acting to which he is so close that he forgets all else. It is their most powerful argument—that the actor's vital force can reach the audience undiminished—and it is a true one, provided the theatre is small.* This brings us with a jolt, however, to the limitations of the actor as a source of communication. He is not a revolving radio beacon. He can give of himself fully to an audience over an arc of ninety degrees by a turn of the head. To cover a wider arc he must use his legs—and find justification for doing so. He can, of course, act with his back, as the enthusiasts like to remind us, but it cannot be claimed that his back is as expressive as his front, and each part of the audience, wherever it is situated, has an equal right to the benefit of the latter. So justification has to be found for move-

* The argument breaks down, for example with a thrust stage as large as that at the Festival Theatre, Chichester. Here there can be no intimacy for the actors, and the dimensions introduce the further complication of acoustical hazards.

ment not in the thoughts and feelings of the character but in the need to dole out the 'important' moments by fair shares to all sections of the audience.

The purpose of this digression into the controversies of theatre architecture is solely to underline the factors that control stage grouping. To sum them up: the *character* needs always to be in the plausible position according to his relationship with the other characters, and to have arrived at that position by plausible means. The *performer* needs to be where the current which flows from him to the audience can flow with unimpaired vitality—and this may well be *upstage* because of the importance of his eyes, but it may well be *down stage* because of the shorter distance; the *audience* wants both these requirements to be met, but it wants its own eyes, in addition, to be led towards the point of attention by the ordinary laws of composition.

Very often these factors conflict with each other, and they illustrate forcibly how often the art of the theatre is the art of compromise. (To deny the need, sometimes, for compromise, to take a rigidly puristic attitude always over styles and methods will too often exclude much of real value.) But there has to be one constant, one factor over which compromise is not possible, and that is the theatrical *truth* for the sake of which all the director's work is done. For example, a director may see in his mind's eye a group of unquestionable theatrical appeal; but he may find it quite impossible to arrive at it by 'honest' means. If that is so he must do without it. Here the ability of modern lighting equipment to come to his aid should be remembered.

There are many books dealing with stage lighting: here the director needs only to be reminded that he has the power to 'paint' his stage with points of varying emphasis, by which means he can compensate, for example, for an unemphatic group. He should remember, however, that unless he does this cleverly he may subject his actors to pools of darkness, in which, if their features cannot be clearly seen, they will be quite unable to communicate. He must illuminate the *actors*, but never the scenery, which will get enough reflected light anyway to make its effect, while throwing the actors into the relief that is their right. Unless his knowledge of lighting is more than adequate he may be at the mercy of the stage lighting experts, which is a bad thing for any director. Nowadays the lighting experts are very expert indeed, but they cannot be guaranteed to look upon a production with objective eyes: they tend to fall in love with effect for effect's sake. It is always best for a director to light his production himself, but if he is unavoidably saddled with a lighting specialist he must know enough about the subject to ensure that he, and not the specialist, is the master.*

* In New York City union rules insist that it is the *designer* and not the director who must light the play. In these trying circumstances it is all the more necessary for the director to be his own expert.

IV · The Intention

IN EXAMINING the different theatrical elements that make up the substance of performance we have seen how these grow out of the meaning to be found in the text. We should now be familiar with them and able to take them for granted. The director does not *think* in terms of these things, but, like any skilled practitioner, he automatically uses his knowledge in the appropriate way. His thinking lies in pondering over his script and getting at the heart of the truth of it *before* he starts his practical work with his actors.

To do this he must of course understand the 'primary' significance of the script, that is, the 'meaning' of the lines of the play in plain print, with nothing added and nothing taken away. This is what would be conveyed by any educated non-performer reading them aloud, and little more than this would emerge if the play were played by a mediocre company with an uninspired director. In the evolution, from primary significance to *realized* significance, the creative power available to the director comes to life. An author's lines are significantly realized only when they are fully felt by the actor—when, in fact, they are 'properly acted'. But it is possible in rehearsals for actors to imagine that they are acting, when they are only 'acting', that is, when they are merely behaving (which is what bad acting is). Bad or false acting usually happens when the performer is not feeling what he is saying. *Feeling* is the operative word. *Thinking* about the lines (as distinct from having an understanding appreciation of what they mean) will not do enough in itself to bring them to life

on the actor's lips (too much emphasis on one of the performer's faculties tends to exclude others: thus thought, to
excess, excludes feeling, while too much emotion obliterates
good sense). It is the same with the director himself: the harder
he thinks the less he will feel, and the better his logic the less
his intuitive sympathy.

To be able to judge that moment in rehearsal when 'thinking' will be of no further use to the actor and when an
audacious improvisation should take its place is part of the
actor's skill. It must be part of the director's, too. He must
know by a sure instinct whether an actor is just saying the
lines intelligently or beginning to feel them properly, and he
must know the exact time, in a schedule of a month's rehearsing, when to apply a gentle flick of the whip and give the
right stimulus to the actor's creative impulses. (Actors, as we
shall see, often want to delay that creative moment to which
they must eventually come. The moment must not have an
induced or premature birth: nor must it be allowed to mis-
carry, otherwise the result will be no better than a skilful
fabrication.)

It is helpful to be reminded at this point of the priority of
emotion over speech in our biological development. Because
we seem to speak with such facility we forget that this ease
is deceptive when assessing man's desire to communicate
through words in relation to his actual achievement in doing
so. One can easily imagine the millions of years of painfully
pointless sounds our species must have made before it finally
acquired the limited vocabulary of the dawn of language.
Certainly there must once have been an enormous gulf,
between man's complex reactions to his environment and his
own kind, and his ability to express them. Now that the whole
corpus of language has evolved and released humanity from
its dumbness there still remain vast tracts of feeling which,
for the ordinary man, cannot be expressed by words, or for
which mere words seem inadequate. So, before the character
in a play can appear to reach for that appropriate word which

appears so ready-made in the script, the actor must have imagined very deeply. Not till he has done this can his 'moment' come. As he may well be a lazy person (plenty of actors are) he has to be stimulated by his director not to think, but to 'feel' what he is supposed to be saying, just as his far-off ancestors once did.

In searching for this feeling behind each line, and in putting it together throughout his part, the actor finds that stream of *inner life** which lies behind the dialogue of so much post-Tchehovian drama. This is the continuous current of 'thought' and 'feeling' which is the character's life-blood. It is in him whenever he is on the stage. It links him up from scene to scene, and keeps him always alive as a character, irrespective of what the dramatist has given him to say. This consistency and continuity when found, enables an actor to build a performance even when the dramatist has lacked the technique which provides the clues. With a dramatist of the quality of Tchehov, the first writer to write plays in which the continuous current is 'built in', it is perfectly possible to trace the inner life of each character from start to finish. But Ibsen is very likely to have thought in a different way, and may have considered his words self-sufficient: the digging out of the meaning behind the Brack–Hedda pauses is not a simple task.

'Inner life' cannot be found in every play in the same degrees. A search for it, for instance, in *The Importance of Being Earnest* would not prove rewarding. The 'linear', classical drama was written with no conscious knowledge of it. To look for it in Shakespeare can prove a fatal trap, since the poetry can be irretrievably lost in a welter of introspective pauses (though there are exceptions to this, as we have seen). The director must examine his script with care to discover what kind of play it really is and then give it treatment according to its kind. The more naturalistic and colloquial

* This is what Stanislavsky's American disciples have labelled the 'sub-text'.

the dialogue, the more likely that it will repay exploration for what is behind it. The more formal and articulate it is, the more certain will it be that the major task of expression is meant to be carried out by the language itself. When the latter is the case nothing but harm can be done by trying to find meaning between the lines instead of in their substance, structure, and rhythm.

With *all* the characters of a play, however, there must be a reason in the actor's and director's mind as to *why* a character has come on the stage and *why* he is taking part in the scene: this is the 'objective' of the scene. If 'inner life' is a thought/feeling current, 'objective' defines the direction in which the current is flowing. Both can be explored in the following scene from Tchehov's *The Wood Demon*.

VOINITSKY: It's difficult, painful. . . . . Never mind. . . . .
(*enter Hroushchov*)
    Later on. . . . . Never mind. . . . . I'll be going. . . . .
(*exit*).
HROUSHCHOV: Your father won't listen to a word. I tell
    him it's gout, and he says it's rheumatism; I ask him to
    lie down, and he gets up.
(*taking up his hat*)
    Nerves!
SONYA: He's spoiled. Put your hat down; wait till the
    rain's over. Will you have something to eat?
HROUSHCHOV: Thanks, perhaps I will.
SONYA: I like to have a nibble at night. There'll be
    something in the sideboard, I expect.
(*rummaging in the sideboard*)
    He doesn't need doctors. All he needs is a dozen
    women round him, gazing into his eyes and sighing
    'Professor!' Have some cheese. . . . .
HROUSHCHOV: You shouldn't talk of your own father
    like that. I know he's difficult but if you compare him

with other people, all your uncle Georges and Ivaniches
aren't worth his little finger.

SONYA: Here's a bottle of something. I'm not speaking
of him as my father, but as the great man. I love my
father, I'm sick of these celebrities, with their Chinese
ceremonials.

(*they sit down*)

What a downpour!

(*a flash of lightning*)

See that?

HROUSHCHOV: The storm's passing us by. We're only
getting the fringe of it.

SONYA: (*filling his glass*)

Have a drink.

HROUSHCHOV: May you live to be a hundred!

(*drinks*)

SONYA: Are you vexed with us because we called you
out last night?

HROUSHCHOV: On the contrary. If you had not called
me out I should have been asleep, and to see you in
the flesh is much nicer than seeing you in a dream.

SONYA: Then why do you look so vexed?

HROUSHCHOV: Because I *am* vexed. There's no one here,
so I can talk openly. How I should like to take you
away from here this minute, Sophia Alexandrovna!
I can't breathe this air of yours, and it seems to me
that you are being stifled by it. Your father, completely
taken up with his books and his gout and with no
interest in anything else, that uncle George, and
finally your step-mother. . . . .

SONYA: What about my step-mother?

HROUSHCHOV: I. . . . . No, I can't speak of everything. . . . I can't. . . . . My dear, there are many
things about people that I can't understand. Every-

thing about a human being should be beautiful—face and dress and soul and thoughts. Often I see a woman so lovely and so beautifully dressed that I'm over-whelmed with delight, but her mind and her thoughts —heavens above! Sometimes a beautiful exterior covers a soul so black that no amount of labour could ever whiten it. . . . . I'm sorry—I'm getting a bit worked up. . . . but you are so very dear to me. . . . .

SONYA: (drops a knife)

Oh, now, look there. . . . .

HROUSHCHOV: (picking it up)

Never mind. . . . .

(pause)

It sometimes happens that you are walking through the forest on a dark night, and if you happen to see a little light gleaming in the distance, your spirits rise and your heart rejoices so that you don't notice your weariness or the darkness or the thorns and twigs that whip across your face. I work from dawn till late at night with no rest winter or summer, contending with people who don't understand me, suffering intolerably at times . . . . but now at last I have found my little light. I won't pretend that I love you more than any-thing in the world. Love is not everything in my life. . . . it is my reward! My dear, my sweet, there is no greater reward for one who works, struggles, suffers. . . . .

SONYA: (perturbed) Please. . . . . One question, Michael Lvovich.

HROUSHCHOV: What do you mean?

SONYA: What I'm trying to say is that your democratic feelings must be offended by your close acquaintance with us. I was educated in one of those schools reserved for the privileged classes, Elena Andreyevna is an aristocrat, we dress fashionably, but you are a democrat. . . . .

HROUSHCHOV: But. . . . really. . . . let's not talk about that! Not now!

SONYA: What's more, you yourself dig peat, plant forests. . . . . It seems so odd. . . . in a word, you're a socialist. . . . .

HROUSHCHOV: Democrat. . . . socialist. . . . . Sophia Alexandrovna, can you really want to talk about such things seriously, even with a tremor in your voice?

SONYA: Yes, quite seriously, a thousand times seriously.

HROUSHCHOV: Oh no, no. . . . .

SONYA: I feel certain, absolutely certain, that if, say, I had a sister, and you fell in love with her and proposed to her, you would never forgive yourself for it, and you would be ashamed to show yourself before your Zemstvo colleagues and your women-doctors, ashamed that you had fallen in love with one of the gentry, a muslined young lady who had never soiled her fingers with work and was always fashionably dressed. I know very well, I can read in your eyes that it is true. It comes to this, in a word, that these forests of yours, and your peat, and your embroidered blouses, they are all a pretence, a pose, a fraud, and nothing more.

HROUSHCHOV: Why, my child, why have you insulted me like this? Oh, well, I'm a fool and I've got what I deserved; I shouldn't push in where I'm not wanted. Goodbye!

(*moves towards the door*)

SONYA: I'm sorry. . . . I was rude. Please forgive me.

HROUSHCHOV: If you knew how stifling and oppressive everything seems here! It is a place where people sidle up to a man and squint at him askance to see if they can discover a socialist, a psychopath, a phrasemonger —anything you like, except a human being. 'Oh,' they say, 'he's a psychopath', and they're satisfied. 'He's a phrasemonger', and they're as fussy as if they'd discovered America! And when they don't understand me, and don't know which labels to stick on my forehead, they blame me, not themselves, and say 'He's a queer fellow, an odd fish.' You are only twenty but you are already old and sedate like your father and uncle George, and I shouldn't be a bit surprised if you called me in one day to treat you for gout. You can't live like that! Whoever I may be, look me straight in the face, frankly, without reserve and without any presuppositions and try to see in me above all things a human being, otherwise you'll never have any peace in your relations with such people. Goodbye! And mark my words, with such crafty, distrustful eyes as yours, you will never love!

SONYA : That is not true!

HROUSHCHOV : It is true!

SONYA : It is not true! Just to spite you I will confess that I do love you! I love you, and it hurts me, hurts! Now leave me! Go away. . . . please. . . . and don't come here any more. . . . don't. . . . .

HROUSHCHOV : With your permission, then. . . . .

(*exit*)

SONYA : (*alone*)

He is angry. Heaven save me from having a temper like his!

(*pause*)

He talks attractively, but how can I be sure that he is not a mere phrasemonger? He is always thinking and talking of nothing else but his forests, and he plants trees. . . . . All very fine, but it's easily possible that that's nothing but psychopathy. . . . .

(*covers her face with her hands*)

I can't understand it!

(*sobs*)

He took his degree in medicine, and now he's completely occupied with other things. . . . . It's all so puzzling. . . . so strange. Lord, help me to think it all out.

(*Enter Elena Andreyevna*)

ELENA: (*opening the window*)

The storm has passed over. How lovely the air is!

(*pause*)

Where's the Wood Demon?

SONYA: Gone.

(*pause*)

ELENA: Sophie!

SONYA: Yes?

ELENA: How long are you going to be sulky with me? We've done one another no wrong—why should we be enemies? Isn't it time we stopped?

SONYA: I too have been wishing. . . . .

(*embraces her*)

My dear!

ELENA: That's better. . . . .

(*They are both moved.*)

This scene seems, at first glance, to employ a very great many words to achieve very little. It is only by a study, in the other scenes, of the characters of Sonya and Hroushchov, that an emotional ebb and flow in it is discovered that is hardly at all revealed by the lines. On examination, the Sonya of *The Wood Demon* emerges as an extremely earnest naïve girl, while Hroushchov is impulsive, enthusiastic and often unaware, in spite of his generous sympathies, of his effect on other people. At the beginning of the scene, Sonya is watchful and expectant, eager to discover what the young doctor's feelings about her may be, for she is in love with him but has been careful not to wear her heart on her sleeve. Hroushchov is attracted by her, more so than he realizes: but when he enters the room he is merely glad of the opportunity of talking about himself and getting her sympathy. This is the kind of indulgence for which any man is ready in the presence of a woman whom he finds rather attractive. His opening lines are therefore something of a show-off—a trifle overdone, to get sympathy. Sonya's first five speeches are charged with an undercurrent of excitement and determination which she is careful to disguise. Her direct question. 'Are you vexed with us', will, she hopes, lead to the answer she wants. His answer could not be more satisfactory, and she is hard put to hide her delight. Hroushchov is quite unaware of the effect his words have had. He did not mean them to have any serious weight, none the less they carried his heart's message without him knowing it: 'to see you in the flesh is much nicer than seeing you in a dream'. As she listens to the two speeches that follow Sonya is tortured by uncertainty: perhaps she interpreted him wrongly after all. But eventually he says 'you are so very dear to me'—the words might mean everything or nothing—and in confusion she drops a table knife. Yet, was she so confused? Such a clear show of his effect on her might well be calculated to evoke some reaction in him, and thence some positive statement. But he doesn't take the hint, he just goes on talking: 'I won't pretend that I love you more than anything in the world', he says blandly, 'love is not everything in my life'. The man has the effrontery to talk to her as if she were not Sonya but someone else! What *does* he want? Instinct tells her that he must love her: it also tells her that he must be punished for treating her so casually. She embarks on a long and involved criticism of him, designed to hurt. What she says is childish: an older man than Hroushchov would have seen through it. He laughs at her naïveté and the prim way in which she flings 'socialist' at him as a term of contempt. But he takes her 'insult' seriously all the same, and goes to the door.

She apologizes: the warmth of her feeling is on the surface now, and she has given herself away. This time the message comes through to him, but he doesn't acknowledge the fact in words: it is his tone of voice which is changed and which betrays the mixture of his feelings. If indeed she loves him then he has made himself look a little foolish. Yet if she does love him that puts her in his power and he can make her a victim of his grievance with justification. Already the relationship of these two is on a new basis: the terrible ability to hurt each other is theirs. He exits at a peak of a quarrel which acknowledges their love.

Sonya's objective at the beginning of the scene is to find out what Hroushchov's feelings are: she has waited in the room for this. His objective is merely to relax and to talk to and impress a charming girl. The 'flow' of the scene is towards this discovery, and the question-mark in Sonya's mind is the same as that in the audience. With the picking up of the table knife the scene has arrived at a point: the question has been answered (though in Sonya's mind there is still confusion). Now the scene takes an unexpected turn. No longer is Sonya being social and charming; she goes into the attack: her objective is to make Hroushchov feel her claws. The 'flow' is towards the answer to the question 'What is going to happen now?' This phase, or 'phrase' (for these divisions, when they are acted, emerge as very like the 'phrases' of a musical score) ends with his move to the door. When he comes back it is he who controls the scene, which flows towards the question 'What is Hroushchov going to do *now*?' With the lovers' quarrel at the scene's end all questions are answered: both the parties, as well as the audience know exactly how they stand.

The scene, we can now see, has broadly followed the formula of the story-teller, the pattern of the song. Expectation (Sonya's probings), suspense (Hroushchov's ambivalent reactions), adventure (Sonya's incursion into attack), recognition (realization that these two love each other) and finality have given *features* to the flow of the scene. Without these, the mere words in performance would have provided only the uneventfulness of their primary significance. Without *shape*, it is now clear, the words themselves have but little theatrical meaning.

The direction of the flow is one of the factors that determine shape. An important climax is often concealed at that point in a scene where the *flow changes*. Take, for example, the following from the tent scene in *St. Joan*. The Earl of Warwick has spent a fruitless half-hour in trying to persuade the Bishop of Beauvais to deal with the Maid the way he would wish: all that has happened however is that these two powerful men have argued against each other:

> WARWICK : . . . Now by The Maid's doctrine the king will take our lands—our lands!—and make them a present to God; and God will then vest them wholly in the king.
>
> CAUCHON : Need you fear that? You are the makers of kings after all. York or Lancaster in England, Lancaster or Valois in France : they reign according to your pleasure.
>
> WARWICK : Yes, but only as long as the people follow their feudal lords, and know the king only as a travelling show, owning nothing but the highway that belongs to everybody. If the people's thoughts and hearts were turned to the king, and their lords became only the king's servants in their eyes, the king could break us across his knee one by one; and then what should we be but liveried courtiers in his halls?
>
> CAUCHON : Still you need not fear, my lord. Some men are born kings; and some are born statesmen. The two

are seldom the same. Where would the king find counsellors to plan and carry out such a policy for him?

WARWICK: (*with a not too friendly smile*)
Perhaps in the Church, my lord.

(CAUCHON, *with an equally sour smile, shrugs his shoulders, and does not contradict him.*)

WARWICK: Strike down the barons; and the cardinals will have it all their own way.

CAUCHON: (*conciliatory, dropping his polemical tone*)
My lord: we shall not defeat The Maid if we strive against one another. I know well that there is a Will to Power in the world. I know that while it lasts there will be a struggle between the Emperor and the Pope, between the dukes and the political cardinals, between the barons and the kings. The devil divides us and governs. . . .

After Warwick's 'Perhaps in the Church, my lord' the bishop considers his position and decides quickly that there is a greater advantage to him in alliance to the Englishman. The direction 'conciliatory, dropping his polemical tone' indicates a sudden complete change of tempo. From the cautiousness of thrust and parry, Cauchon now becomes brisk and determined, since he has made up his mind. The whole scene quickens, and continues thus to the end: it is as if, up to this point, the objective was being painfully approached uphill, while after it the descent is quick and easy. This effect can only be achieved if the thoughts of the characters are understood and the value of tempo changes in indicating objectives perceived.

Sometimes even when the greatest care has been given to the elucidation of inner life, there is a hidden 'key idea' behind an entire scene. The scene may be fully expressed by the director in all its aspects, *except* the one vital aspect on which it really depends. The key idea has been left out because it has not been perceived, and the true point of that scene is consequently lost:

(*Finally Varya enters, looking for a long while at the luggage*)

VARYA: Strange, I can't find it anywhere. . . . .

LOPAHIN: What are you looking for?

VARYA: I packed it myself, and I can't remember.

(*pause*)

LOPAHIN: What are you going to do with yourself now, Varya Mihailovna?

VARYA: Me? I'm going to the Ragoulins. I've arranged to go and look after them—as a sort of housekeeper, you know.

LOPAHIN: Aren't they at Yashnevo? That's forty miles away.

(*pause*)

So life in this house has come to an end. . . . .

VARYA: (*looking among the things*) Where can it be? I suppose I must have put it in the trunk. Yes, life has come to an end in this house—and there will be no more—

LOPAHIN: And I'm just off to Kharkhov—by the next train. I've a lot of things to do there. But I'm leaving Yepikodov here. . . . I've taken him on.

VARYA: Good gracious!

LOPAHIN: This time last year snow had fallen, if you remember, and now it's quite fine and sunny. It's a bit cold, though—three degrees of frost.

VARYA: I haven't looked.

(*pause*)

Anyhow, our thermometer's broken. . . . .

(*pause*)

A VOICE FROM OUTSIDE: Yermolai Alexeivitch!

LOPAHIN: (*As though he has long been expecting this call*) Just coming!

(*Exits himself*)

(*Varya, sitting on the floor, lays her head on a bundle of clothes, and sobs quietly.*)

This scene from Act IV of *The Cherry Orchard* is one of the most familiar in the Tchehovian canon. It is a halting scene, with a number of pauses (more than are indicated in the script: one after Varya's 'I must have put it in the trunk', the other, particularly important, before 'This time last year the snow had fallen'). The pauses, of course, help the actors to indicate the suppressed feelings which give the scene its fuel. Varya's sentiments for Lopahin would flower into love if she had the slightest encouragement—indeed perhaps she loves him already, though we may be sure she has never said so. This meeting between them among the piles of luggage, before the Ranevsky house is left for ever, seems to her to be her last chance to attain her heart's longing. Yet she is hoping against hope. Lopahin's rather blundering efforts sincerely to do what Liouba has told him—to offer Varya marriage—takes a comedic colour. It is a typical example of the Tchehovian counterpoint, where the feelings of one character in a scene are strongly contrasted with the feelings of another, so that both emotions are set in vivid relief by their juxtaposition.

If the performers of both characters have professional ability and play with honesty, he making conversation but with concern in his voice for his own awkward predicament, she doing the same, but with difficulty concealing her true thoughts—much of what is implicit in the scene will come through to the audience. And when Lopahin leaves the room, so obviously using 'the voice from outside' as an excuse to get away from her, Varya's tears will have the complete sympathy of the audience.

But, so far, the core of the scene is lacking. However well the performers act, and however well they have established themselves in the earlier scenes, the desolation of Varya at the end will do no more than to leave the audience mildly affected, unless the key idea is there. Without it the scene will have achieved nothing, since there is nothing that the scene 'tells' the audience that it doesn't already know.

The key idea is simple: it is the idea of *hope built up, only to be destroyed.* If the way the scene is played kindles *hope* in Varya's heart, however little, and if this is allowed to grow in her, then, when the hope is dashed with Lopahin's exit, the scene has a story to tell: the pattern of question/ suspense/answer is there. And so the director must not work the scene as if Lopahin knows the way it is going to end. He must not interpret Lopahin's seizing the excuse of the 'voice from outside' as meaning that he was not, at least, *trying* to propose to Varya as Liouba wished him to. Lopahin, in fact, *tries hard* to bring himself to the point of asking the question. Underneath her lines Varya is aware of his painful efforts, and the more painful they are, the more she thinks (though she hardly lets herself dare think it) that he may after all declare his love. During Lopahin's pause after 'that's forty miles away' her hope strengthens, and though what he says next ('so life in this house has come to an end') is disappointing, it can be construed by her as possibly a preliminary to something more exciting. She does not, in fact, abandon hope until the very last moment. She is, of course, at war with herself: one part of her is warning her that Lopahin is not going suddenly to change into a different man, while the other, the optimistic half, is telling her that miracles can happen.

The actress must play the scene as if this tension would tear her to pieces. Hope starts to ebb when she exclaims 'Good gracious'. He merely refers to the temperature. 'I haven't looked,' she says, with difficulty keeping up her conversational tone. She pauses after this to give him a last chance to speak from his heart. But Lopahin, though he has done his best, cannot go through with it. 'Anyhow, our thermometer's broken', she says, as her hope fades completely. She just, but only just, manages to hold herself from breaking point while he is in the room. The call 'Yermolai Alexeivitch!' is almost as great a relief to her as it is to him. Lopahin rushes out, and, left alone, Varya slowly subsides to the floor.

The whole scene has the quality of tragedy. But it is also ridiculous and full of laughs. That is Tchehov's way.

Images of the past can sometimes be magical elements of theatre; the echo effect is a favourite with writers (Nina in Act IV of *The Seagull* is perhaps the most famous example in drama) and a director can use it with powerful effect. There can be either poignancy, or mystery; there can be irony, too, in the pattern that recurs, though such echoes should be sparingly used (a production containing more than one or two would seem self-conscious). At the right moment, however, the evocation of an image can increase the profundity of the emotion with which it is concerned.

There is such a moment in *Macbeth*.

But first, a digression. The interpretation of Lady Macbeth involves considering a certain principle. It is a principle which I shall call that of harmonic discord: that is, certain kinds of characters can only be truly realized in depth, provided the more obvious elements of which they are composed are combined with other elements which are, apparently, contradictory to them. There are dramatic parts such as Goneril, or Iago, or Lady Macbeth, which are so written that they are extremely highly charged, and can therefore easily become melodramatic when acted. Much can be lost, and nothing will be gained, if they are cast with performers who already possess those dominant qualities with which the author has endowed them. Thus the wise director does not choose a 'ruthless' Goneril, a 'sinister' Iago, or a 'cruel' Lady Macbeth, but picks the very reverse. The reason is simple: if an actor adds personal characteristics beyond his own control to characteristics which are already present in the script, he will create a surfeit of dominant qualities and the resulting excess will not be believable to an audience. If, on the other hand, the actor himself is quite 'different' from the part he has to play the two contrary elements fuse harmonically to create a character in depth. That character becomes 'real' precisely because he is made up of opposite elements in the same way as people are in life.

The principle of harmonic discord does not apply merely to casting. It appears in the creation of many characters from Shakespeare's onwards. It flows in the lifeblood of Lear and Hamlet, of Ophelia and Peer Gynt and Hedda Gabler.

It can also be built into the basic conception of character-interpretation by director and actors. Lady Macbeth is not only a monster of wickedness. She is also a warm-blooded woman with a passionate loyalty and love for her husband. Her very imprecation that she be unsexed and filled 'from the crown to the toe with the direst cruelty' suggests that she was once no stranger to the softer emotions. If she is to be acted in depth the actress has every reason to seek vulnerability among her attributes: the echo effect will help her to express this, and, it will also help her to bring weight to the part in the last half of the play—just where it needs this most.

In Act III, Scene 2, she realizes for the first time that something has gone wrong:

> Nought's had, all's spent,
> Where our desire is got without content:
> 'Tis safer to be that which we destroy
> Than by destruction dwell in doubtful joy.

In this scene she comes to realize that Macbeth's feeling for her, which once flowed so powerfully, has ebbed to nothing. Later she says to him:

> Gentle my lord, sleek o'er your rugged looks;
> Be bright and jovial among your guests tonight.

If any clue were needed for a director to understand what ties this husband and this wife together, the reminder is here : there has been a physical passion so strong between them that for its sake Macbeth has allowed ambition to corrode all that was once in him of honour, wisdom and humanity. But now the price has to be paid, and the first instalment is Macbeth's forfeiture of the fiery comfort of sexual abandon that his wife's embraces once provoked so easily. She embraces him here—she can scarcely do less, if the words are to evoke the appropriate action. She does so with the full force of the sexuality which bound him to her in the past. Macbeth, a subtler creature than his wife, suffers earlier than she for the enormity of their crimes; her caresses mean nothing to him. He is already no more than a husk; we know he 'will sleep no more'. The hot embrace goes cold before our eyes: in this moment, provided only that Lady Macbeth is permitted to possess *vulnerability*, the director and the actress can provide a glimpse of what her hell will be.

After the banquet scene Lady Macbeth is off stage for a very long time, and when she reappears, her sleep walking scene is extremely short. It is easy for an actress not to be memorable here, because of the lack of the necessary stage time in which to re-establish herself with the audience. To fail to be memorable in the sleep walking scene, however, is virtually to fail altogether. The director has a duty to her and to the play to avoid this if possible, and one way he can do so is by the echo device. If he can connect the sleep walking scene not only with the time of the murders *but also* with a time long prior to that when tenderness could still prevail, the limitations of this short linear scene can be avoided. The abortive embrace in Act III, Scene 2, has already shown that there was once a real passion between husband and wife. Is there a place in Act V, Scene 1, where the audience can be reminded of this? If so, the scene is immeasurably strength-ened, since there can be no stronger emphasis of the present than to contrast it with the past. Examination of the sleep walking scene reveals one place in it, and one place only, where this can happen. It is shortly before her exit. The reference to all the perfumes of Arabia has just been made:

DOCTOR: What a sigh is there! The heart is sorely charged.

GENTLEWOMAN: I would not have such a heart in my bosom for the dignity of the whole body.

DOCTOR: Well, well, well. . . . .

GENTLEWOMAN: Pray God it be, sir.

DOCTOR: This disease is beyond my practice—etc. etc.

Up to this part of the sleep walking scene the point of attention ought to be fairly shared by Lady Macbeth with the two watchers. She of course is the dominant figure, but the Doctor and the Gentlewoman are also important, because they represent the world of sanity and compassion. Also, they have pertinent things to say. The dialogue is so spaced that it is easy for the audience to concentrate first on her and then on them and to get the full value from both. The places where she moves will have had to be carefully chosen. She cannot move while the Doctor and the Gentlewoman are speaking without reducing their importance to nothing. Yet she must move, she must enter and depart, she must deposit and pick up the taper, she must do the business of washing her hands: it is 'her' scene, and it is a sleep *walking* scene. These actions should be aptly performed between the lines. But now come five consecutive speeches of comment which leave Lady Macbeth, as an actress, conspicuously unemployed. (The director may have had difficulty in restraining her up to this point, for the scene well represents the duality of theatre, the tension between what the actress feels the character would do and the actual theatrical implications of the scene *in toto*. What follows, in addition to having great value for its own sake, would be likely to compensate her for restraint up to this point.)

Her restraint must continue during these five speeches. Lady

Macbeth stands absolutely still until the Gentlewoman's 'Pray God it be, sir'. That line marks the end of a phrase, a finish, since there is really no further comment necessary from the two watchers. Yet the Doctor goes on, 'This disease is beyond my practice—' etc., and his comment is not short. There can be no reason for him to continue unless Lady Macbeth does something new and strange in the wake of what she has done before. This is her opportunity, this is the place for the echo-effect.

Suddenly the doctor is riveted by a new expression in Lady Macbeth's eyes. His companion follows his gaze. They stand stock-still and watch, and the point of attention comes swiftly on to the sleepwalker. To their amazement, she seems no longer mad: her eyes are full of love; the hot passion of the past is with her again. She is embracing a phantom figure, repeating almost exactly the rhythm of her arm movements as she made them in Act III, Scene 2. Her caresses call to mind a time long before that banquet scene, a time before the slow death by corruption of their love. Just as before, the embrace dies into emptiness: she, and the audience with her, are now again at that moment before the banquet scene: the echoes of the distant past and of only yesterday are vividly impressed upon the present. Her eyes go dead as the vision fades. It is 'now'. Her Hell is in her eyes and she is mad. The echo is over and the Doctor speaks his amazement and horror: 'This disease is *beyond* my practice'.

There is something again to be said about pauses, and what can lie behind them. Once a character has become deeply entrenched in an audience's consciousness, and has *experienced enough*, a pause in the right place becomes a reservoir of many feelings and emotions that he has so far been unable to put into words. Then, concentrated as they are, and provided the actor has enough imaginative intensity, these thoughts and feelings, if invited by the director, will speak

D

for themselves. It is as if the reservoir can contain just so much before the dam breaks and the contents pour out: or, to change the metaphor, it is like a cloud which grows steadily more ominous, until the surfeit of electrical charge within it makes it crack in thunder.

Consider Solonyi's single entrance, to speak a mere ten lines in Act IV of *The Three Sisters*. Those lines are deliberately trite, yet their realized significance is charged with feelings which, true to his character, Solonyi is quite incapable of expressing in words. Beneath their cover he suffers a frustrated romantic desire for Irina, a hunger for the respect of his brother officers (which has always been denied him) and a craving to be thought an intellectual by the people he meets. Over the scene there hangs a pall of fear; it is a fear of death in the duel he is just about to fight. But also in the picture that Solonyi has imagined, with himself as the central figure, is the idea of a holy sacrifice, of a hero prepared to do and die for his goddess.

All this is behind the words of the scene, but it is more than the best of actors can convey in the time covered by the lines. The stage directions say that after it Solonyi and Tchebutikin go out to the duel together. But if Tchebutikin can be made to exit alone, not looking back to see whether the other is following him (as the nature of the Doctor's feelings would undoubtedly suggest) then Solonyi can have his moment. It is in fact far more than a moment. Left alone at this point of crisis, he can invest that pause with almost all that he has ever longed for and all that he has ever failed to achieve. When the dam of the reservoir 'breaks', however, it must break into action. And the longer the pause, the greater the supercharge, the more compulsive the action.

In the case of Solonyi, the action, since he is clearly obsessed by Irina, is a kiss blown at her window. But it can be a long time, as he stands there, before he need do anything at all (*expectation and question-mark as he stands there— maybe before going to his death*). Then at last he moves to below Irina's window (*question-mark and adventure: what is going to happen now?*). He blows the kiss. It is an action normally associated with gaiety and inconsequence, and in this context it therefore gains markedly in significance (*question-mark and relaxation: can this kiss have any result? But no; no such kiss in this play can have any result*). His hand drops. He struggles with his tears. He pulls himself together, resumes a soldierly uprightness, and goes (*finality*). The pause has become a scene in itself.

It could be argued, of course, that to create such an acting sequence as the above is to gild the lily, and to encourage the actor to indulge himself. Assuredly this pause could, in theory, give opportunity to a cheap actor for an unprecedented exhibition of vulgarity. Yet the 'opportunity' has in it a built-in safeguard. Solonyi's last moments in the play can contain no more than Solonyi has already put into the reservoir throughout the preceding Acts. The empty actor—and what is a vulgar actor but one whose technique so outstrips his imagination that his performance can have no content—would be afraid to hold the pause for longer than a couple of seconds.* The imaginative actor, on the other hand (though his taste would cause him to approach the opportunity with caution) would be fascinated by the challenge, and, under directional guidance would soon make it his own.

'The greater the supercharge, the more compulsive the action'. This is to say that the more goes into a pause the more powerful is the impulse towards action that occurs within it. And therefore, the more powerful is the action. With Solonyi the power is compacted into the intensity of the kiss: unless that intensity appears behind all that Solonyi does, his 'moment' is meaningless. Later in this Act the point is illustrated in a different way. Irina has just heard from the Doctor those fatal words 'the baron has just been killed in a

---

* When Livanov of the Moscow Art Theatre played Solonyi in Nemirovitch Danchenko's production, his pause before this exit held the audience successfully for a minute and a half.

duel'. To which her immediate reply, in the script, is 'I knew it, I knew it— (*weeps quietly*)'. No actress and no director can leave it at that. The shock of the Doctor's statement clearly indicates a pause for Irina before she can find the words with which to react. It is another 'opportunity' for a sensitive actress, but it is a very difficult one indeed. She is stunned by the bald statement. But when she emerges into full consciousness of the brutal *fact*, what does she do? Delicate restrained acting, however 'true' can have no place here. 'Acting from the belly' (an ability to express elemental grief usually and wrongly associated solely with foreign performers) becomes imperative. The power that Irina has generated and stored throughout the play must burst the flood gates: it breaks out in a cry of animal pain. If the power is as great as it can be, a mere discharge of sound is not enough to carry it: the force of emotion spills out into movement, and Irina sweeps *upstage* for twenty feet before coming to rest.

Now, be it once again noted, *Irina cannot do this unless she has genuinely built up that supercharge in the reservoir of her emotion.* This is why it is useless for a director just to tell her to do it:* he must help her, indirectly, to find so much inner feeling during the preceding Acts that it will come quite naturaly not to flinch at the necessity here.

There is an interesting area of speculation concerned with the timing of the outburst, after the pause which precedes it has begun. *Before* a certain point, as we have already seen, neither the audience nor Irina can possibly react (the audience has itself to digest the Doctor's announcement before it looks at Irina to perceive what it means to her). *After* a certain point it will be too late for Irina to do anything at all: she

---

* In Nemirovitch Danchenko's production Stepanova swept up stage exactly like this. But when a younger actress of the Moscow Art Theatre eventually took over the part, she was directed (by another director charged with keeping the production in being after Danchenko's death) to perform precisely the same evolution. She was unable to do this with conviction, despite her ability: her emotional reservoir was not full enough.

will have passed the moment at which her outburst is plausible, and there is nothing then that she can do without being unreal or holding up the flow of the play. Between these two points lies the latitude which theatrical truth presents to the actress, and which gives her individuality full scope. But within that latitude she has still to obey the logic of the part's emotional situation. The longer the actress waits before making the outburst the more will be expected of the outburst itself: it will have more anguish, more depth, behind it. But if a less experienced (though still emotionally true) actress takes the hurdle she will be able to satisfy the audience with a more modest effort *provided she has burst the dam sooner.*

Thus the quality of a performer can affect the way stage movement and grouping are done: since emotion discharges itself through movement, and movement can take the actor to where the director would like him to be. Nothing better illustrates the duality of theatre, the interdependence of actor and director, the interdependence of feeling and mechanism, than this situation where Irina's tragedy can be used to establish the appropriate grouping of the sisters by the fall of the curtain.

Consider the following from Act I of *The Seagull:*

ARKADINA: A good idea, but don't let's talk of either plays or atoms. It's such a glorious evening. Can you hear the singing?

(listens)

How lovely it all is!

POLINA: It's coming from the other side of the lake.

And the following from Act IV of the same play:

MASHA: . . . When we are gone I shall soon forget it all, —tear it out by the roots.

(*Two rooms away, a melancholy waltz is being played.*)

POLINA : That's Kostya playing—he must be feeling depressed.

Music is the off stage effect in each of these quotations from *The Seagull*. In the first case the sound of singing from across the lake is in a way quite irrelevant. It does not spring from any of the characters, and the events of the play could happen in exactly the same manner if the director were to excise it: it would merely be necessary to cut two lines. In the second instance the music is a persistent reminder of a *fact*—the fact that Konstantin is only just in the next room. To the other characters this fact is something to be taken for granted, but to *us*, the audience, it is Tchehov's intention that Konstantin's frustration, his unhappiness, his essential lack of a justification for living, should be frequently emphasized: not only does the author want him emphasized, he wants the theatrical thread that Konstantin represents woven into the tapestry of the scene.

Thus an effect can do two things, or both of them together. The singing across the lake in the first Act draws attention to nothing definite other than the existence of a life going on outside that small section of it under the dramatic microscope. But in reminding us of the continuity and omnipresence of life in general it serves to emphasize the vividness of what is *before our eyes*. Konstantin's heaviness of heart, Masha's disillusionment, Medvedyenko's mediocrity, Polina's yearnings, Dorn's cynicism, Nina's capitivation with life, Trigorin's caution and Arkadina's egotism are all given an extra sharpness by it—provided the music is of the right kind and that its volume, and consequently its degree of compulsiveness, are properly gauged.

The piano music in Act IV equally heightens what is going on in the scene itself, and lends colour to Dorn's hedonistic pleasure in existence, to Polina's silent endurance, to Medvedyenko's general uselessness. But in this case all the threads are pulled by the music into one single knot—the tragedy of Konstantin himself—provided, again, that the music is appropriately managed.

All off stage sound effects (for music is only one of the kinds of sound which can affect atmosphere on the stage) are, generally, either discreet, calling attention not to themselves but to the existence of another plane of being; or they are explicit, postulating a certain definite importance for a certain definite purpose. And both kinds depend on appropriateness of *kind*, and preciseness of *control*.

For example, the singing across the lake after the débâcle of Konstantin's play should, of necessity, be vague of outline, with no marked features to make the audience want to listen to *it*, instead of listening to the dialogue. It should not underline any particular emotion, since the emotions expressed by the characters on the stage are of so many different kinds that to emphasize any one of them would be to do so at the expense of that mosaic-like quality which the scene obviously requires to have expressed. Yet it would clearly do its work best if it could provide a strong contrast to what is being said and done on the stage. This could only be if what is sung off stage flows against the emotional tide of what is happening on stage. Appropriate music might therefore be some jolly sort of a popular song, except for the fact that jolly popular songs tend to have an angularity of outline which is more than likely to intrude upon the lines. And so, perhaps a sentimental tune is indicated, since long and flowing (and therefore unobtrusive) phrases are characteristic of these. There is another reason for such a choice. Sentimentality is romanticism with reality extracted from it. The resulting unreality not only emphasizes, by contrast, the truth which is happening upon the stage, it also subtly points an ironic finger at the romance of the setting itself—the lake, the moonlight, the wooded glade where the stage is set for Konstantin's play. And thus it underlines the illusory nature of all Nina's feelings in her present immaturity. (Incidentally a sentimental song is also what holiday makers on a lake on a moonlight night are rather likely to sing.) But the volume at which the singing pervades the action is an equally important factor. The audience should hardly be conscious of it except when Arkadina draws attention to it: then it must seem to float in on the fitful summer breeze, sometimes softly audible, at other times almost felt rather than heard.

Konstantin's piano-playing in the next room is the other kind of effect. It is specific in character. It is meant to be actively listened to, though not for long: sometimes it, too, takes on the character of what is vulgarly called 'mood music'. Again, control of volume is important: the notes dominate the dialogue at times, and when they do so their volume swells and the characters listen to them. At other times they are soft enough to be forgotten, and the dialogue happens over them. Here, because the music refers to Konstantin and is supposed to be played by him, it obviously must be appropriate to his own mood. But it should never be a well-known piece recorded by a professional pianist: a Chopin study, for example, is immediately recognized as such, and if the audience is reminded, by the evocative power of music, of personal emotions or memories, then both director and actors will be wasting their efforts. The ideal piano piece then is an obscure work with the right qualities (and of appropriate period) or, better still, a sensitive and specially composed pastiche, which can be carefully tailored to the lines.

Both these examples of sound effects are specified by the dramatist himself. But occasions abound where the author has left it to the director to discern where such comment is of value. As a general rule Shakespeare's plays need music only where Shakespeare has specified it. But with the undistinguished material of *Titus Andronicus*, Peter Brook achieved great directorial distinction partly because of the electronic accompaniment, which he himself composed.

Sometimes a felicitous use of music can spring from the

words of a dramatist who had no such idea in mind. When the comparatively inexperienced Tchehov of *Ivanov* specified a 'cello as being on the stage in the last Act, he probably thought no more than that a great country house prepared for a wedding party would show all sorts of evidence of forth-coming jollity. The 'cello would be seen by Shabelsky on entering, and this would very naturally give rise to Shabel-sky's tears as he is abruptly reminded of his dead musical partner. Tchehov had not yet achieved the mastery of his medium which would have enabled him not to drag that 'cello in, *only* to give opportunity to a character to express himself. The sophisticated Tchehov would have given it a context. The sophisticated Tchehov would have realized that music could give the unity his last Act needed: moreover, he would have seen that this same music possessed the power to bring the play to a consummate finish.

The director can start to build this effect (which culminates in the final curtain) from the very beginning of the Act, if he shows not only a 'cello on the stage, but other instruments as well. They are at the back of the set, together with the musi-cians' chairs and music stands. At the beginning of the scene between Lebedyev and Sasha the musicians enter and prepare to tune up. Lebedyev, exasperated that he can find no privacy for the talk he so urgently wants with his daughter, tells his servants to lead them out of the room. Their unwilling de-parture adds its quota to the turbulence in Lebedyev's mind. The Act proceeds. Later, Ivanov has a tempestuous scene with Sasha which continues with gathering and relentless momen-tum for a considerable time. However well the part is played Ivanov here is in danger of becoming a bore: his diagnosis of the situation is worthy and well meant but his demented persistence is on the verge of becoming ridiculous, and it can-not somehow be taken seriously. *Something is needed to show the audience that it can laugh at him if it wants to.* The trigger to do so is provided by the musicians who, as soon as he is well launched into his first tirade return to get their

D*

instruments. For a moment or two they stand, watching, fascinated by the extraordinary performance, yet completely uninvolved and detached from it. Then they make a dash on tiptoe for their fiddles and go. But Ivanov has not noticed them and goes on talking: comedy has entered,* and his seriousness is now framed in farce. The play continues, the guests begin to gather, and still Ivanov goes on talking. From next door the faint sound of the fiddler practising arabesques can be heard; the tempo of his rapid arpeggios seems to mock the rhythm of Ivanov's words. More guests gather, the musicians off stage begin to tune up: their efforts seem to be building towards some sort of climax—and the denunciation scene† is doing exactly the same thing. Although they are not thinking about it the audience is subconsciously aware that the musicians are almost ready for their moment, the moment when they will do what they are paid to do and burst into triumphant music. The final scene speeds towards its climax: Ivanov too is approaching his moment, the moment when he is to be supremely himself. The tuning up ceases as Sasha pours out her contempt for Ivov: the musicians are forgotten as the Act approaches its end, which has already been described, on page 43.

Stage effects, musical or otherwise, need to be used with care. They can effect a director like a drug and cause him to fall in love with his own ingenuities. Here is part of a notice of a production of mine of *Uncle Vanya*.‡

Mr Fernald, apparently giving up his actors in despair, concentrates on the play's rural atmosphere and gives us highly convincing bird songs and farmyard grunts and cacklings. But the pace tends to be over-sluggish throughout, and even the lightning in the second act's thunderstorm is noticeably slow, as lightning goes.

* See Chapter V on Comedy.
† See page 53.
    ‡ Alan Dent: *News Chronicle*, March 1952.

This punishment was well deserved. It goes to show how easily a small matter like Marina calling her chickens can lead a production to disaster.

That moment when a director is in danger of losing his priceless objectivity is something he must be able to recognize. It can easily take him unawares, because, since it is part of his function to anticipate elements which will be pleasing to the audience, he must himself *like* the treatment which he accords to the play under his charge. It is very natural to extend Marina's chickens to a background of farm noises, for the soft sounds of geese and rooks, the lowing of distant cattle and the cooing of doves make, in theory, a perfect background for the sultry first Act of *Uncle Vanya*. As rehearsals develop the director, who has fallen for what has seemed to be magic, will be more and more beguiled at the effect on himself of such strands of sound, delicately and subtly interweaving with the dialogue. He will note too—and this will seem to confirm to him that he is going the right way about things— that his effects are making his actors *act better** (and this will not be illusion, but the truth). So, congratulating himself on the success of his pastoral sound-plot for the first Act, he will perforce deal logically with the succeeding Acts. The possibilities of the storm in Act II will be ranged exhaustively, black-birds will be mercilessly exploited in Act III. By the time he has reached Act IV, where an occasional nightingale in the deepening dusk can vividly underline the heart sorrow from which so many of the characters are suffering, and where the guitar music and the harness bells specified by the author are a 'must', the fatal damage has been done. Sound effects, as a theatrical element, have cheapened in value : they have become at their least worth at precisely that point where they should be at their most important. That is the crux of the matter : sound effects, magical though they are when spar-ingly and aptly used, can all too easily become the stalest of theatrical clichés. The wise director has this warning written

* See Production Practice, page 150.

on his heart. If he ignores it his actors may be blamed for what is no fault of theirs.

But the beneficial value of effects on actors, provided, of course that their volume is low enough to be no impediment to dialogue is a factor very much to be reckoned with. Sound effects touch off the imagination of performers, and it is very often at that moment when they are introduced into rehearsals that rehearsals begin for the first time to come alive. Before the director lets himself fall in love with such effects, however, he should remind himself that the level of volume which allows the actor to become inspired is almost certainly one which would be completely inaudible to the audience. And he would be wise therefore to allow any effects that are not essential to phase themselves quietly out of existence as rehearsals develop. They will then have done their work on the actors and the actors will not miss them. Neither will the audience.

An acid test of an effect is whether or not it satisfactorily answers the question 'Does this add anything to the production, which, without it would be the poorer?' If the answer is not an unequivocal 'Yes', then the effect should be scrapped. But equally acid is the test of aptness. Stanislavsky wrote to Tchehov as follows, when he was working on Act II of *The Cherry Orchard* for the first time:

> Will you allow a train to pass by, puffing smoke, during one of the pauses? That might be very effective. Toward the end we are having a fog: it will rise toward the ditch at stage right. The concert of frogs comes at the very end.

Stanislavsky's desires for *The Cherry Orchard* were, in my opinion, execrable, hardly worthy of one who knew the importance of 'the feeling of true measure', and who coined that admirable disciplinary aphorism for the guidance of artists. But Stanislavsky was clearly swept away by the sense of his own power. As he certainly was when he proposed to

have Tusenbach's body carried across the stage at the end of
the last Act of *The Three Sisters*.* These errors of taste, with
possibly others as well, were aborted by the absolute firmness
of Tchehov himself, but nowadays where is the dramatist who
could challenge a director on this, his acknowledged field?
Protection against the vice of self-indulgence subsists only in
the director's own innate honesty. And in his proper appreciation of his place in the scheme of things. His job is not that
of a decorator, nor of a virtuoso, juggling with his material in
order to draw attention to himself. His work is to deepen and
to clarify a vision which an author has already seen: it is to
that vision that he must apply all his perceptive and creative
powers. If he cannot do this, he is nothing.

* See *My Life in the Russian Theatre* by Nemirovitch Danchenko,
Geoffrey Bles, London, 1937.

V · Comedy

CONSIDER THIS, by Gayev to Varya in *The Cherry Orchard*:

GAYEV: Yes. . . . If you find a lot of different treatments recommended for some disease, that means it's incurable. I've been thinking and racking my brains, and I've got all sorts of plans—ever so many—and that means, really, not a single one. Of course it would be nice to have a legacy from somebody, or it might be a good idea to marry Anya to some rich man, or we might even pay a visit to Yaroslavl and try our luck with my aunt the Countess. She's rich, you know, really wealthy.

VARYA: (*crying*) If the Lord would help us.

GAYEV: Now, don't whimper. Aunt's rolling in money, but we're not in her good books, unfortunately. My sister, to begin with, married a provincial barrister instead of a gentleman. . . . .

Examination of this passage shows it to be a typical piece of Tchehovian self-revelatory dialogue. Gayev is seen as a more complex character than the sleepy, vague and prejudiced sentimentalist so far exhibited in Act I. He is humorous, and sees the joke of himself; he is shrewd about other people, recognizing the faults of his sister, for example, without the slightest malice: yet he cannot curb his optimistic fantasies, which are completely at odds with his sense of realism. Gather up these qualities, add to them the other discoverable characteristics such as talkativeness, tenderness, laziness, self-indulgence, patience, impatience, tolerance and intolerance, distil the lot into life through the imaginations and techniques of first class direction and acting, and there one has the sum of the ingredients necessary for a performance of Tchehov's Gayev . . . but one has nothing of the kind. One has it very very nearly—which (since the theatre is the harshest task-master) is scarcely better than not having it at all. For a vital element is missing.

What is missing is the quality of Comedy—the one ingredient which is indispensable since it is an ingredient without which most dramatic writing, even though skilfully executed, cannot endure from one generation to another.

We know Tchehov to have been profoundly aware of this, as the greatest of writers have always been. We know Gayev to be both a comic and a serious character at the same time (for this was ever Tchehov's way). But where exactly is it to be found in this passage—and surely if it is inherent in a fully rendered Gayev it will have to be found here? This is as good a train of thought as any from which to start an excursion— a modest excursion, for the subject is as wide as Drama itself —into the realm of this mysterious and necessary force which is behind so much that is written by playwrights, and is the key to so much that is spoken by actors.

The clue-sentence in the inventory of Gayev's character-istics is, of course, 'his optimistic fantasies are *at odds* with his sense of realism'. For it is a truism that comedy springs basically from a disparity of one kind or another provided it is large enough. The joke of Gayev is that he approaches the extremity of self-contradiction, and is far too lazy to make any effort to solve the problems that this poses. For him the dream, and its inevitable corollary the deflationary truth, co-exist in one and the same moment; but not being a fool he needs but a glimpse of the resulting inconsistency to be in full retreat towards sweet-eating, or thoughts about snooker, or any fancy that will serve to cover up something he doesn't like. The kernel of the joke is the dichotomy between optimism and pessimism, and the fact that Gayev is equally definite about both.

That kernel is clearly expressed:

'I've been thinking and thinking and racking my brains, and I've got all sorts of plans—ever so many—*and that means, really, not a single one.*'

The obvious trap is to fail to see the joke in the way the lines are written, and so, inevitably, not to realize that its effect subsists in how the actor treats the sentence in italics. For the 'acted joke' depends on conveying the following sequence: a feeling of true compassion and a genuine desire to help in the initial attitude to Varya ('I've been thinking and *thinking*') which climbs towards limitless goodwill ('and racking my brains') and climbs further to a plane where 'plans' can be equated absolutely with achievement. With 'ever so many' the kindly uncle is on a peak of expansiveness: but now, so to speak, Gayev must be rushed willy-nilly downhill to reality, as if he didn't quite know what was in his path. There is the briefest of pauses, and then with a sudden gear-shift from expansiveness to its extreme opposite of utter matter-of-factness, comes the pay-off, '*and that means, really, not a single one*'. The trick is in the pause and the change, which could be expressed crudely thus:

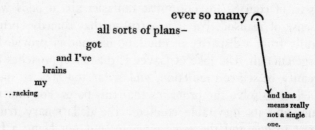

(The crescendo suggested by the rising and expanding print is *not a crescendo of volume, nor, necessarily, a rise of pitch.* It is an intensification of sincere assertion. '⌒' represents the pause, a mere taking in of breath. The small print at the end represents the suggestion of a dropped voice and a de-flation towards matter-of-fact statement.)

If director and actor follow this pattern, doing so of course with the full thought behind it and not merely expressing its tone/tempo superficialities, the result will be a comedy reaction from the audience.* It will be obvious, however, that understanding in the actor will not by itself achieve the result without the corresponding technical treatment. The following way of saying the line, for example, will not do the trick:

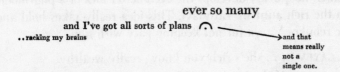

The tone/tempo contrast expressed by this shallow graph is not enough to convey the degree of Gayev's optimist/pessimist dichotomy.

This way will not do, either:

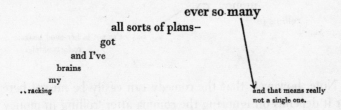

* I prefer this phrase to that of 'getting a laugh'. The aim of every comedian is to get a laugh, and the laugh he gets is a comedy reaction. The wider the aim of the dramatist, and the consequent scope of the material, the more is it possible that the comedy reaction may not consist of audible laughter, that it will, so to speak be no more than a 'smile in the brain'. The actor, in contra-distinction to the professed comedian, is not necessarily trying to get laughs: he is trying to explore and convey each of many facets of the character. In the course of achieving this he will get some big laughs, some little laughs, and some smiles in the brain. All of these are comedy reactions, and all of them, even the latter; subtle though they may be, are noted by the sensitive actor's antennae.

To elide the reverberative and deflationary pause '⌢', as we have seen in Chapter III is to fail to separate sufficiently the two contrasting ideas, and thus to fail to hit the nail on the head with the first idea before abruptly shifting gear to the second: again the necessary degree of contrast is lost.

Now, as we pursue Gayev further we find the pattern repeats itself. He pauses for reflection after 'not a single one'. But such is his resilience that he is soon off on a fresh flight of fancy about marrying off Anya 'to some rich man', from which he quickly develops the even better idea of a pilgrimage to the rich aunt in Yaroslavl. This idea really takes hold and he rebukes Varya for not keeping pace with him:

GAYEV: . . . she's rich you know, really wealthy.

VARYA: If the Lord would help us.

GAYEV: Now don't whimper. Aunt's rolling in money, but we're not in her good books, unfortunately.

Here is the same joke again, but stronger:

Note, however, that the comedy can easily be missed here, for it depends on ignoring the comma after 'rolling in money' and turning it into the '⌢' or full stop. (Ignoring of punctuation in the script is often necessary, and there is nothing sacrosanct about the commas and semi-colons of the dramatist. These have not always been put there as an indication of how a line should be spoken and are quite often no more than unconscious literary gestures.)

The joke-pattern is now set. Gayev goes on to criticize his sister for being the cause of the aunt's disapproval, and his loquacity is flowing nicely when Anya enters unobserved, and Varya admonishes him for casting aspersions on her mother in front of her. Again he pauses, '⌒', brought up short. He realizes his fault, is highly embarrassed, and tries to absolve himself with a quip:

'It's rather strange, you know, but something's happened to my left eye.'

But his sense of guilt persists as both girls tell him that he talks too much. He shies off his vision of himself into an even more preposterous flight of fancy:

GAYEV: But there's just this little matter of business. Last Thursday, as I said, I was on the Bench, and I got talking with the fellows there about one thing and another, and it seems I might be able to fix up a loan on a promissory note so that we could pay the interest to the bank.

VARYA: If the Lord would help us!

GAYEV: When I'm there on Tuesday, I'll mention it again. (To Varya) Don't whimper. (To Anya) Your mama will talk to Lopahin; in the end he won't refuse her. And as soon as you're rested up you can go to Yaroslavl to your great-aunt the Countess. So there we are, you see, with three good plans, and one way or another the business is as good as settled.

Three of the vaguest, most remote hopes conceivable, one of which Gayev himself exposed as useless, are triumphantly paraded as glorious certainties. Gayev's character is established for the rest of the play.

The type of comedy just examined is what that great *Times* critic of a bygone age, A. B. Walkley, used to call 'the comedy of apt characterization'. It can be found wherever the lines provide a suggestion of opposing, contradictory elements: in the best writers it is easily discoverable in the words themselves. But, very often, quite ordinary material can be found to provide opportunity for the same comedic treatment, for it must be remembered, it is *what the voice does with the lines* that produces the comedy reaction, rather than the lines themselves. (It should be needless to add that tricksy voice changes unbacked by the sense would be dismally unfunny as well as untrue.)

The careful director, then, combs his script for paradoxes and unlikely associations, and it is astonishing what he may find. His reward can be a deepening in the characterizations of his actors, their gratitude, and the gratitude of the audience.

'Comedy of apt characterization' is a phenomenon which stands aside from the rest of the subject of comedy. It belongs to the entire range of naturalistic theatre, being like a trace element or seasoning, which though a separate and definable element, pervades the whole and becomes incorporated with it. It is an additive, an enricher, whereas the other sort of comedy, the kind which, for instance, is conjured up in our minds when we think of Congreve, Oscar Wilde or N. F. Simpson, happens as the result of a reduction process, in which certain aspects of 'reality' are blanked out for the greater emphasis of what remains. 'Apt characterization' sets the final seal of truth on an actor's portrait, adding a flavour of the unexpected which is a part of life, and which is ever a reminder that, despite the natural order, chaos is only just behind our shoulders. It is built up in rehearsal, tenderly and gradually, out of dozens of little touches and afterthoughts, and it is a process that can continue through progressive rehearsals for some considerable time, continually enriching a performance—provided it is always treated as a natural and organic process, and not something to achieve which dialogue and acting generally are being over-strained. It is something which calls upon every part of an actor's abilities, and for that acting which is unspoken just as much as that which is spoken.

Moreover, it is such a powerful element that the expression of it can sometimes make the written word superfluous. When the doctors in *The Doctor's Dilemma* each in turn recount how Dubedat has swindled them of various sums of money, Sir Cutler Walpole turns to the Hebraic Shutzmacher, and the author's direction is economical:

WALPOLE: Did he get anything out of you, Mr. Schutz-macher?

SCHUTZMACHER: (*shakes his head in a most expressive manner*).

The cunning Shaw well knew that a good actor, provided he has fully and deeply already expressed Schutzmacher's character, would never be allowed by the audience to get as far as saying 'No'. The timing of the shake of the head, how-ever, is the key to making the point, if it is to provide the full comedy reaction that is implicit. A quick 'straight' shake will achieve little, but a pause of incredulity at such a question, while the expectant doctors gradually realize the extent of their own gullibility will bring the house down the moment Schutzmacher's head begins to move.

But now it is time to consider the opposite of this kind of comedy, and to examine some aspects of what is sometimes referred to as 'true' or 'pure' comedy, with the entirely differ-ent range of problems that arise therefrom.

Here is part of a scene from *The Cresta Run*, by N. F. Simpson:

A Soho alleyway. Same. Leonard, dressed exactly as when he left the house in the previous scene, has been cornered by Andreyevsky, who has a suitcase full of large brown envelopes open on the floor, and is offering one to Leonard.

ANDREYEVSKY: A bargain, really. At the price. Hardly used.

LEONARD: Yes. Not a bad size, I suppose. Anybody wanting that size.

ANDREYEVSKY: Nice weight, too. Feel it—in your hand. Not too small, not too big.

LEONARD: Yes. I see what you mean.

ANDREYEVSKY: Sell a lot to those Connoisseurs and people.

(*pause*)

One of the best sizes they bring out. In my opinion.

(*pause*)

Sold a treat in Ancient Greece that would have done.

LEONARD: It would?

ANDREYEVSKY: Oh, yes. Not too long, not too broad. They'd go for that. Classical, you see.

LEONARD: Ah.

ANDREYEVSKY: Like the Parthenon. Ever see the Parthenon?

LEONARD: No, I can't say I have.

ANDREYEVSKY: Beautiful size.

LEONARD: Yes?

ANDREYEVSKY: Not too long, not too broad. That's what does it, you see. Proportion. Length against width.

LEONARD: What are you asking for this? If it's not a rude question.

ANDREYEVSKY: Two guineas.

(*pause*)

They were hot on anything classical in those days of course.

LEONARD: Yes. . . . I . . . .

ANDREYEVSKY: Give them anything that wasn't classical and they wouldn't look at it.

(*pause*)

One of the things they're noted for. The Ancient Greeks. More than anything else.

(*pause*)

Tradition.

(*pause*)

That's why they'd have gone for that, of course.

LEONARD: You think they would?

ANDREYEVSKY: Buff envelope that size! They'd have gone mad.

LEONARD: Really?

ANDREYEVSKY: They'd have been fighting in the streets for it.

LEONARD: Yes. Well. . . . .

ANDREYEVSKY: If I turned up in Athens with that envelope I'd have been mobbed.

LEONARD: I wonder. . . . . Before I settle for it, I wonder if I could by any chance give it a trial. . . . .

Here we are back in linear theatre: this dialogue must be considered and acted from the point of view of the words, and nothing but the words: naturalistic reality is emphatically not what must motivate the thoughts of actor and director here. Simpson is depicting a world where two utterly disparate aspects of human behaviour co-exist in a manner which is actually impossible—therein lies the necessary 'disparity which is large enough' for comedy to happen. Those aspects are on the one hand, the middle-class clichés of modern commercial intercourse, and on the other the classical concepts of the architecture of Ancient Greece. Projected to their logical conclusions these bring about a discussion about the Parthenon and a brown business envelope in a perfectly natural manner as though it were possible to apply identical standards to each, and the monstrous premise, that there can be an aesthetic argument about a brown envelope at all, is taken completely for granted.

Such is the extravagance of this idea, and yet such is its delicacy, that the wrong direction of it, and consequently the wrong acting of it, can tumble it into a shambles of non-acceptance by the audience. The actor must present nothing to them but the idea itself, expressed with the utmost simplicity, by an appropriate personality. Any attempt to do more will break the tenuous cord which connects comedy with life and cause the scene not to be believed and therefore not to be laughed at. Nothing in the way of playing it must be a reminder of the actuality where such a discussion would be impossible: actor's clichés in the way of 'heavy acting', 'putting the lines over', excessive pointing, excessive stage business, excessive use of facial expression, must be ruthlessly ruled out. The only world the audience can be aware of is the world of Simpson fairyland, where the envelope-seller with the gift of the gab is as natural a phenomenon as a strip tease tout in Soho.

What can emerge from the scene is a delightful picture of the timeless struggle betwen the archetypal salesman trying on his confidence trick and the archetypal customer determined not to be done, but losing the battle just the same. The picture is delightfully simple because, presented this way, it is *fresh*, and the audience therefore looks upon what is actually a commonplace situation with an eye so new that it seems original and yet at the same time attractively familiar.

Timing here is the actor's prevailing means. A pause before 'Anybody wanting that size', as Leonard, the hero, cagily puts up his guard. A longer pause before 'sell a lot to those connoisseurs and people', as Andreyevsky appraises his victim and trots out his tactics: the gradual dropping of Leonard's guard as he becomes caught up in the temptations of snobbery as the dialogue begins to gather momentum. Leonard is a lost man as he quickly plunges in with 'What are you asking for this?' And he fights a delaying action, with the tentativeness of '. . . I wonder . . . before I settle for it, I wonder if I could by any chance give it a trial. . . .' And so on.

The rhythm of the lines is so felicitous that the words trip off the tongue. The stresses naturally fall into the right place.

None but the veriest amateur should fail to make these lines work provided they are just left to happen audibly *with the right thought behind them, and nothing else.* It is this uttermost simplicity, this austerity almost, that provides the trap for the unwary, for it seems to suggest the opposite of that detailed synthesis of life which it is the actor's especial talent to create. In fact, it is an exceedingly salutary discipline for both director and actor. And it will not appear to be excessively difficult, provided certain facts about comedy reactions are ever borne in mind.

To begin with, it has to be realized that the 'reduction process' by which the comedic essence is distilled, is not only part of the technique of presentation: it is also inherent in the audience's attitude. It is an attitude of detachment. Comedy, it has been said, is 'Tragedy viewed from afar off' whereas tragedy can only be felt if the audience becomes closely involved in it. It is as if the audience, in submitting to laughter, and in placing itself in a position where it is prepared to submit to laughter, is voluntarily freezing certain of its instincts in order to stimulate others. Bergson said of the comic that 'to produce the whole of its effect . . . it demands something like a momentary anaesthesia of the heart. Its appeal is to intelligence, pure and simple.'*

The state of mind of an audience watching a comedy is an extremely critical state of mind. Unblurred by any emotion, always a possible obstruction to clear thinking, it is in a unique position to perceive the manner of a performance as well as its matter; for that reason all the *formal* aspects of performance of comedy assume a very great importance, and such qualities as neatness of movement, economy of gesture, clarity of diction, an easy-flowing manner of speaking, smartness on the cues and all other excellencies of technique need to be present in perfection. With a more naturalistic type of play failures of perfection in the manner may often be compensated for by a great sincerity in the expression of the

* See *Essay on Laughter* by Henri Bergson.

matter. Such distractions as false emphases, clumsy speaking or moving may be forgiven by an audience which is emotionally disposed to accept sincere acting: for, while an audience is engaged in some emotional reaction it is not in the least interested in technique, provided that technique is not sufficiently bad to hinder the emotional effect. Moreover, it may say, such clumsiness does after all happen in real life: how many people really speak well; how many are able naturally to move gracefully?

But pure comedy is the most artificial of the conventions. In it we are rarely asked to look upon life: we are asked to regard a world entirely separate from life which has its fascination precisely in that separation. The people of comedy neither act, speak nor behave as real people do. They make no mistakes of diction, they move always at the right moment and their very gesture and expression is always a perfect reflection of the situation in which they find themselves. If they have emotions, they are emotions from which we in the audience are removed. We regard them quite dispassionately: tears in comedy move us to laughter.

This lack of emotional intent behind the lines of comedy means that the time required for an audience to react to them is less; for the minds of an audience are quicker than their emotions. Therefore the general tempo here will be quicker than in other types of play, and each character will for the most part speak smartly on his cues. Pauses will, of course, occur, but their purpose will mostly be for the registering of comedy points, for obtaining and 'feeding' laughs, and for planting material for laughs at later stages of the play. The general impression of the performance must never be one of slowness, for if an unnecessary pause occurs there can be nothing during its occurrence to which the audience may react. Deprived of all emotional content, which might give an audience something to ponder over during the gaps, comedy dialogue must have the continual stimulus of pace if it is to keep alive.

An important aspect of the creators of comedy is that they partake of superhuman qualities. Within the field of their own discipline they exhibit a perfection unattainable by ordinary men. In this the actor of comedy resembles a ballet dancer: he has developed a superlative facility in a particular direction, and only another of his own kind can emulate him. She who plays Millament has a control of her tongue, lips, and breathing apparatus which enables her to speak extremely complicated and artificial sentences as if they were the most natural 'throw away' lines—and to do it without the appearance of the slightest effort, like a remarkably delicate machine. It is this hint of an effortless mechanism operating inside a human being that actually creates the comic ambience and informs the audience just where it stands. Bergson referred to it as a 'mechanical inelasticity' and laid it down that laughter inevitably occurred whenever it was present. Certainly the 'machinery' does not necessarily have to be complex, as in Congreve: what is necessary is that it should persist with obstinacy, that it should present the image of a rigid inexorability in contrast to the flexibility of the life around it. 'Mechanical inelasticity' is the basis of many a comic character and many a comic situation. This excerpt from a French farcical scene, where a soldier-husband with only one idea in his head calls in on his home in the course of a devastating retreat, shows how it operates.*

(*Hannibal, alone once again with Sophie, becomes suddenly practical.*)

HANNIBAL: Now, no more talk.

SOPHIE: You are going?

HANNIBAL: No. You are coming with me.

SOPHIE: Where to?

HANNIBAL: To our room.

* *Les Derniers Outrages* by Robert Beauvais, Cahiers du Théâtre, Paris, 1953.

SOPHIE: Hannibal, you don't mean it!

HANNIBAL: Why not?

SOPHIE: There's a war on.

HANNIBAL: The war can wait.

SOPHIE: But . . . in the middle of a battle. . . .

HANNIBAL: The only battle that interests me at the moment is the battle I propose to win in my own house, under the canopy of my own bed.

SOPHIE: It's not there any more.

HANNIBAL: What isn't?

SOPHIE: The canopy. . . .

HANNIBAL: Why not?

SOPHIE: It was moth-eaten. I had it taken away.

HANNIBAL: Then I will do without it. Come.

(*He moves towards the bedroom door.*)

SOPHIE: Are you mad?

HANNIBAL: I am at war.

(*He holds out a hand. She does not budge.*)

You refuse to do this for your husband? . . . Then do it for a soldier. Do it for your country.

SOPHIE: Positively and absolutely—no!

HANNIBAL: A fine patriotic spirit! Stop arguing, woman. If it hadn't been for your shilly-shallying it would all be over by now—or very nearly.

SOPHIE: (*frigidly*) Kindly do not introduce barrack-room manners into my house.

HANNIBAL: I see. I shall have to use force. After all, I am master here.

(*He approaches her. She retreats. Enter Sophie's mother from the kitchen.*)

SOPHIE'S MOTHER: There's some cold ham on the kitchen table; potato salad and gherkins.

HANNIBAL: Will you get out?

SOPHIE'S MOTHER: Lord, he is badly shocked.

HANNIBAL: I am not in the least shocked!

SOPHIE'S MOTHER: Well, as long as somebody isn't. . . .
(*She disappears into the kitchen again.*)

HANNIBAL: (*urgently*) Quick. The enemy are upon us.
There is not a moment to lose.

SOPHIE: (*obstinately*) If that is so, your place is at the
forefront of our army.

HANNIBAL: I swear I won't take my hand off my sword-
hilt.

SOPHIE: Go!

HANNIBAL: (*through his teeth*) So be it. You refuse yourself to me. I shall take you by force. I shall set you
aflame with desire.
(*He stalks her round the room.*)

SOPHIE: (*retreating*) Hannibal!

HANNIBAL: You shall shudder with longing. You shall
faint, you shall drown in an ocean of passion.

SOPHIE: What is the matter with everybody today?

HANNIBAL: (*arrested*) Everybody? What do you mean by
everybody?

SOPHIE: (*realizing her mistake*) Nobody. . . .

HANNIBAL: Ha! Too late! Tell me all!
(*He seizes her wrist.*)

SOPHIE: I am confused. . . . I don't know what I am
saying. . . .

HANNIBAL: You said everybody. So there are several!
How many! Tell me! I must know! Who? Who?
Who?

SOPHIE: (*violently wrenching herself free*) Very well. I
refuse to try and save you from yourself any longer!
Anybody! Everybody! Anybody you care to name!

HANNIBAL: Let me see. It must be someone under sixteen

... or someone unfit for military service ... ah, that's who it is, some coward with flat feet, limping around filching your honour behind my back. ... Oh, the devil damn this war, that kills every soldier twice! ... Own up! Confess! How did it happen?

SOPHIE: (*moaning*) Don't ... don't. ...

HANNIBAL: You have betrayed yourself, there is no going back. ... Tell me, how many times?

SOPHIE: Stop, oh, stop. ...

HANNIBAL: Where did it take place? Here? In a field? God of mercy ... in a field! Down among the grasses and the treacherous wild thyme, where no husband's honour is safe! ... What did he say to you? How did he go about it? Whisper it, word for word. ... No one shall know but we three. ... Did he coax or command? Was he silent? Did he persuade you by force, or by logic? Or by gentleness? That was it! Gentleness! I knew it! Gentleness always succeeds with women. I should have warned you. This tragedy need never have happened. ...

SOPHIE: But. ...

HANNIBAL: (*bellowing*) Woman, I too shall be your lover, out there in the tall grass! I can be gentle too!
(*He seizes her roughly.*)

SOPHIE: For pity's sake, Hannibal. ...

HANNIBAL: (*hissing in her ear*) At least you have been discreet? You have told no one? At least you have not forgotten that between you and this man there hung the shadow of. ...

The reader who has reached this point will not require a detailed analysis of the salient aspects of the scene. Hannibal's drive, his jealousy, his obsessiveness—to be expressed in a pressing, relentless tempo—provide the regular beat of mechanical elasticity. In contrast to this steady rhythm is the flexibility of Sophie and her mother, both of them, compared to Hannibal, recognizable wayward and fallible humans. The interruptions by Sophie's mother serve to emphasize the main rhythm by deliberately interrupting it and exacerbating the temper of the comic character.

There is a noteworthy extension of the mechanical inelasticity idea which can be noticed. This is the 'comedic irrelevancy' effect, whereby characters in a comedy, who are obsessed by the seriousness of their own situation, treat matters which are irrelevant with exactly the same degree of emphasis as if they were vitally important.

HANNIBAL: The only battle which interests me at the moment is the battle I propose to win in my own house, under the canopy of my own bed.
SOPHIE: *It's not there any more.*
HANNIBAL: *What isn't?*
SOPHIE: *The canopy. . . .*
HANNIBAL: *Why not?*
SOPHIE: *It was moth-eaten. I had it taken away.*
HANNIBAL: *Then I will do without it.* Come.

The six lines I have put in italics must not, in the playing, be treated as the parenthesis which in fact they are. On the contrary, they partake of precisely the same urgency, and are acted with precisely the same degree of pressure, as the main flow of the scene. The speculations about the age of Sophie's supposed lover, and the botanical background of the imaginary incidents, have the same quality, and must also have the same emphasis.

Incongruity—the unnatural linking of dissimilar ideas, and their treatment as if they were appropriate to each other—this is another source of comedy:

HANNIBAL: You refuse to do this for your husband? . . . Then do it for a soldier. Do it for your country.

The Bergsonian concepts of inelasticity, of the impingement

of something mechanical upon life, and of incongruity beyond the normally acceptable, are all clues for the director of funny plays. Their verbal expression has its counterpart in corresponding action, or vocal interplay, and every one of the theatrical elements we have examined can be used, therefore, to create Comedy. But woe betide the director and actors who have failed to acquire the technique with which to do it, since Comedy is the most difficult of all the acting conventions. It is difficult, not only because of the extra-critical state of mind of the audience which watches it, but because comedic method itself demands an especial nimbleness and control in the performer. This is scarcely surprising: if the semblance of mechanical smoothness (modified, needless to say, by the waywardness, in opposition, of human personality and imagination) is a fundamental requirement of Comedy, then the actor must be capable of acting with the *efficiency* of a machine. Efficiency means a flexible control of the way the machine is used. Many a comedy reaction is lost because actor and director between them have failed to gauge the appropriate dynamic of a line or an action—and in this, of course, the performer is on a tightrope. If he does not hit hard enough there will certainly be no comedic effect. On the other hand, if he hits too hard the failure will be even worse, for then the disaster, as well as the reason for it, will be impossible to conceal.

Comedy can really be successfully produced only after a very thorough knowledge has been obtained of the general principles of ordinary theatre work. Then, success may depend, paradoxically, upon the degree to which those principles are forsaken. Sir Alec Guinness once said: 'To do anything really well in the theatre you've almost got to forget how to do it, sometimes'.

That was a wise remark. Its application to comedy is that it rams home the fact that careful imagining, reverent attention to the reason why, and assiduous observance of principles (such as those, for example, which govern the dramatic pause)

can, when the desired effect is Comedy, completely destroy it.
It is the *unexpected* in comedy that so often creates laughter.
To ignore the logic of an appropriate pause, or even sometimes
to speak a line with (apparently) thoughtless glibness can
create a result which could never be won by obeying the rules.

And yet, paradoxically, rules really do exist in comedy, and
there is a mathematical precision about them. When we read
Alice in Wonderland we enjoy the White Queen's conun-
drum:

'What's one and one and one and one and one and one
and one and one?'

And we delight in Lewis Carroll's eccentric comic sense. Yet
an actress playing the part of the White Queen will not
achieve a comedic effect by speaking that line as written,
however well she does so. But she will get a laugh, and a
gratifying one, if she adds an extra 'one and one', *counting to
herself (and of course silently) a beat of four before doing so.*
The breaking of the established rhythm of the 'one and one'
is what causes the effect: the audience first thinks that the
Queen has finished speaking, and is then pleasantly jolted
into surprise to realize that she has not. The beat of four is
the precise and necessary beat to do this. A beat of three will
still possibly manage to get the laugh, but the effect will be
weaker, while a beat of five will give too much time for it
and this will cause it to fade away altogether.

This particular joke will be seen to be due to a combination
of the 'mental inelasticity' and the 'sudden and unexpected
incongruity' ideas incorporated into a single packet. There is
nothing like insurance, even in theatre.

So what do director and actor do, faced as they are with the
inconsistencies and contradictions which present themselves
in spite of that precision and certainty which is such a feature
in the making of comedic success? They can only rely on
their own pious faith in their own personal comedic sense.
They can only examine the script for those places where there

E

is a hint of the possibility of 'the mechanical impinging on life', or where there may be variants of the incongruity effect which could be properly developed. Examples, particularly of the latter, are many: one character in a play, for instance, may act in one convention while his opposite is acting in another (John Worthing's funereal appearance in Act II of *The Importance of Being Earnest* gives a clue to the playing of the scene with *Jack* which can transform it, as far as its comedic quality is concerned, from a comparatively dull duet to something which is very funny indeed). Then there is the joke where the *audience shares information with a character which the other characters* do not possess:* this is a situation always to be looked for, since its effect, if comedy is sought, is certain. Then there is the 'ruined climax' effect: the actor builds to a climax, then he or one of the others who are playing the scene 'spoils' the effect by denying it the weight and grandeur which a serious climax positively needs to have. Fundamentally the director has to rely on thoughts and ideas that make him laugh, and then he must have faith that he can cause his audience to laugh too. He can ensure that his faith will be justified if he takes the joke to pieces and finds out why it is funny. Then, in putting it together again, he can see to it that it is played accurately according to the particular principle that it exemplifies. But if he does not discover the structure of the joke his failure is likely, and eventually, after a number of performances in which the vagaries of the human element have had time to play their part, that failure will be certain.

* That remarkably successful modern comedy, *Relatively Speaking*, by Alan Ayckbourn, is entirely based on this idea.

VI · Attitudes and Interpretation

THE ATTITUDE OF THE DIRECTOR towards his material should
be one of love. It is difficult not to feel impatient at the
thought of a director who despises the play in his charge: he
can learn so much from even the most indifferent material.
What is more, he can contribute so much to make it better.
He can take hold of dialogue that is literally unspeakable and
turn it into lines that actors can say. He can deepen and
develop an author's incomplete ideas and create a continuance
of thought and feeling for the actors to express, where the
author had conceived of no such thing. Provided he does not
deceive himself into believing that he has transformed a
mediocrity into a masterpiece there is scarcely any limit to
what he can do in making something out of nothing—and
his actors, who have their livings to make and cannot always
choose the plays they will act in, will even be grateful to him.
(Actors owe a debt to bad authors. One reason that English
performers are regarded so very highly in the western world
is that most of them have served an apprenticeship in poor
plays, and have consequently been forced to work their
imaginations and all their creative faculties doubly hard in
order to make their material theatrically viable.)

Every play script has a potential of communicability, which
waits for the discernment of a director to make contact with
an audience possible. It is as if the script emitted signals which
a director, because he is a director, can pick up. The signals
may be weak or they may be strong, but to a good director
they should unmistakably be there, and he should be able

131

to recognize them. It seems to me essential that he should possess the sensitive antennae with which to do this, yet I am surprised at how often directors have achieved success while seeming to fail in this respect. This, I think, is because there is a comparatively easy way to success—success measured in terms of recurring opportunity rather than artistic achievement—if a director chooses to serve himself first and the play second. In serving himself, in drawing attention to the clever way he uses the means at his disposal, he is betraying both his author and his actors, but he succeeds all the same in very effective self-advertisement.

I think there can be no disservice to Shakespeare in interpreting *The Tempest* in the way suggested in Chapter I. But what is to be thought of a *Tempest* where Prospero plays his opening scene with Miranda in front of a translucent perspex surround, of a pattern so charming, and so intricate, that the eye can never leave it? Where Ariel enters to the sound of a dozen cracking whips, as a section of the perspex breaks from the main structure and clatters to the floor to let him in? Where Caliban comes onto the stage with a four foot bone held before him at an angle indicative of sexual excitement? (As if the scene that follows did not adequately convey his proclivities!) And where the masque is enacted by no less than six goddesses—an Iris, a Ceres and a Juno, composed of perambulating straw effigies, fourteen feet high, out of whose skirts appear yet another Iris, another Ceres, and another Juno, who do the duty of actually speaking the lines? What might certainly be said of such activities is that they were conceived by a director who did not care about Shakespeare's words. Yet they were all of them to be seen at a world-famous theatre only a few years ago. and they were no doubt applauded by the undiscriminating audiences who saw in them effective examples of clever direction. But of course they emphasized this directorial element at Shakespeare's expense; no actor can successfully compete for an audience's attention with irrelevancies of this kind.

The strongest signals emitted from a play by Shakespeare, and the easiest for any director to pick up, are those which say that the subject matter is expressed by words and nothing else, chosen for their sound as well as their meaning, and arranged, for the most part, in a definite rhythm. Such signals are too obvious for the director whose attitude is not that it is a pleasure to be given the opportunity to direct Shakespeare, but merely that the interpretation of him is something in which the important thing is to avoid all theatrical ploys that have ever been used before. But to do what is new and original is not necessarily to do what is right. A director should bring a questing mind to his work, yet he should seek inspiration on the level of the dramatist's chosen method, otherwise, to the discerning, he will fail to measure up to the quality of his material.

The attitude is all important. In Ibsen's *Hedda Gabler* the director's attitude can be both inquisitive and sceptical, yet if he also has respect and regard for the genius of Ibsen, his enquiries can lead to a level of performance not always reached with this play. Unaccountably, *Hedda Gabler* is usually presented as a melodrama, in which a cold-hearted woman who has failed to pull off a number of unpleasant plans for the discomforture of people whom she is unable to treat decently, at last commits suicide, to the great satisfaction of everybody in the theatre. An original director can be sceptical about the usefulness of such an interpretation, and inquisitive about what Ibsen was really trying to do. He can note that the play is a tragedy, and that the classical definition of tragedy is something which in 1890 Ibsen was scarcely likely altogether to flout (although his way of expressing it would be modern in relation to his time). He might therefore conclude that somewhere in connection with Hedda's character the concept of nobility is discernible, since some suggestion of nobility would be a necessary attribute in a tragic heroine. He could discover therefore that tragedy might spring in Hedda from the contrast between her potential qualities and her achievements (where it could never spring out of the failure of a disappointed and scheming woman to achieve a number of selfish objectives) and would set to work to find out what such potential qualities might be. He could discover that Hedda had a great many attributes which, had they been able to develop in a way denied her by her social and historical situation, would have grown into the qualities of a classic heroine. She was beautiful, intelligent, possessed of humour, even of wit; she was fastidious in her tastes and gifted with a personality and magnetism greater than those of anyone around her. She surely had it in her to be courageous —yet that is exactly what she was not. Could she in happier circumstances have shown a capacity for real love? It is an enthralling question, which repays the kind of research into character that director and actress must make together. One answer to the enigma of Hedda—and it is a productive answer —is that because she is so intelligent she is fully aware of all her potential qualities; more than that, she is aware of the gulf between these and their fulfilment. That is her tragedy. It is borne of the knowledge that by the rule of *noblesse oblige* noble conduct should be hers: yet she will never, can never, achieve it. If the actress who plays Hedda shows that the character has in her a large measure of self-awareness—instead of doing all she does from a blind animal instinct—there is classic appropriateness about her end, not futility. And her 'is there nothing I can do?' to Mrs Elvsted, not long before she shoots herself, should hit the audience between the eyes with its tragic implication.

If the director can regard his material with affection and excitement (this should be easy enough with dramatists of high quality) he can be led not only to avoid obvious pitfalls in the script but also to look in it for qualities which are not always apparent at first glance. To take Bernard Shaw: any director should be able to note that the famous Ibsenite, despite his description of *Heartbreak House* as 'Fantasia in the Russian Manner' was unaffected by the Ibsen–Tchehov revolution, as far as his own plays were concerned. They are 'linear' plays, depending for their effect on the brilliant prose of the dramatist, and demanding superlative verbal technique in their interpretation.

Yet this is not the whole truth. Most of *Heartbreak House* and some of *St Joan* show a side of Shaw rather different from the picture of himself that he liked to show the world. Until he wrote the former he had maintained the fiction that his head ruled his heart. He had no use for the romantic notion of theatre, with its stress on feeling as a prime mover of plot. He had no respect for the theatrical weaver of spells, yet this is what he showed he could do in both these plays. It is as if there was war inside Shaw: the artist of the theatre, with an artist's interest in character and an understanding of emotions which he had not himself experienced, was in conflict with the political preacher and pamphleteer. The perceptive director will look for the paradox and express it. He may see that the last Act of *Heartbreak House* contains more than some of Shaw's finest dialectic: that, for instance, Ariadne's lament for the absence of horses in Shotover's establishment is not only exceedingly funny but also in her self-revelation, strangely moving. He may think that the whole play is in fact about the central conflict of Shaw's artistic personality, and see it in terms of the struggle between Intellect and Emotion. (If he does he will not go far wrong. This conflict is an important element in a number of the plays: it is dominant in *The Doctor's Dilemma*; it is behind much of the comedy in *Arms and the Man*; it is a powerful factor in *Man and Superman*, and also in as different a play as *You Never Can Tell*.) In *Heartbreak House* there is an understanding and a preoccupation with human feeling which has often surprised the critics—although this may well have been the emergence of a Shaw more real than the Shaw he liked to show.

MANGAN: How can you have the face, the heart—
(*He breaks down and is heard sobbing as she takes him out.*)

LADY UTTERWORD: What an extraordinary way to behave! What is the matter with the man?

ELLIE: (*in a strangely calm voice, staring into an imaginary distance*) His heart is breaking, that is all.

(*The Captain appears at the pantry door, listening.*)

It is a curious sensation: the sort of pain that goes mercifully beyond our powers of feeling. When your heart is broken, your boats are burned: nothing matters any more. It is the end of happiness and the beginning of peace.

When Ellie says this to Shotover she suddenly lays bare her heart: she gives the lie to the self-possession which, on the surface, has made her seem unnaturally controlled. But the line, of course, is a clue to how the whole part can be tackled. All the characters in this play reveal their vulnerabilities at certain points, and all of them can convey a feeling in contradistinction to their words. Yet the words and their phrasing still remain the most important thing about them. Shaw's characters are articulate and fluent to a point far beyond that justified by outward reality. How then exactly does the director convey emotion between the lines when the characters are not 'human' yet express 'human' feeling? He may be tempted to break the lines up and to fill the interstices between them with gestures, business and many unconscious actions. People do such things while they are 'thinking' hard or 'feeling' hard, or when they are trying to express themselves. But Shaw's characters are not 'people'. They are channels for the communication of what Shaw wished to say. In *Heartbreak House* the emotion of heartbreak fills Ellie Dunn entirely, and must be powerfully felt and understood by the actress. It is 'real'. But Ellie herself is not real: no real girl, even in 1920, ever found it so easy to hit on exactly the right words at all times to say what she wanted. Her perfection of prose, forceful yet with an odd touch of pedantry, belongs to the *essence* of a kind of youthful femininity we can recognize, but it does not belong to any girl fully clothed in the context of reality. So a naturalistic interpretation of the character will not do. What is needed is concentration by director and actors on the full significance of the words and their rhythm. Shavian actors must, more than most, know and understand all that they say. And, above all, they must *really* think before they speak—and give more concentrated attention to this necessity than with any other type of drama.

The artifice of Shaw—and the fact that he knew audiences would only listen to his ideas if he seasoned them with comedy—makes it all too easy to distort his plays. A director may be tempted to let the comedy drift into farce and, because the characters are not 'real' in the naturalistic sense, to throw away the warmth of feeling which nearly always can be found at their centre. He must maintain his directorial balance, the more so since Shaw did not always do so himself. The epilogue to *St. Joan* exemplifies the problem. Many people regard this as a blemish on an otherwise fine play, whereas if the balance between feeling, dialectic, and comedy has been maintained from the very beginning, it is seen for what it is, the play's crowning glory. To achieve balance it is necessary to cut intelligently and without fear (there are many places where too many mocking shafts hit the same target too often). But more important is the need for discretion in the acting of the comedy so that the audience is ready to take serious things seriously when they come.

Where Shaw demands feeling as well as dexterity, lightness as well as staying power, Brecht also imposes an endurance test on the actors, and is equally taxing on their vitality. But the weapons he uses to dominate his audience are heavier and more cruel. Where the foreignness of an Ibsen or Tchehov play is only a part, and a not very important part, of the total atmosphere, the foreignness of a Brecht play permeates the whole and the director must not forget it. The universality of Brecht will only be apparent if the director remembers that he was German and that he wrote in a particular histori-

E*

cal context. Politics as a rule make for dull drama. Brecht is an exception to the rule. The politics he professed for most of his life must be in the forefront of the director's thoughts no less than the violence of his emotional bias. His sympathies in all his plays are expressed with crudeness to the point of naïveté, but the simplicity is deceptive: on top of it he builds a dialectical structure of remarkable complexity. His way of writing, made no easier by the problems of translation, does not help an inexperienced director to follow the twists and turns of his thinking. With no playwright is interpretation more dependent on the director finding the climax and point of each scene, each part of a scene, each 'phrase' and sub-phrase.

Apart from getting the meaning clear, the style must be conveyed. Absence of style results in milk and water Brecht, and nothing can be worse. The dramatist was forcibly feeding his audience and nothing can be achieved by ignoring his propagandist nature on the grounds that conditions at home have nothing in common with the climate of Brecht's own country and epoch. Our Anglo-Saxon audience can be temporarily transformed by the magic of the theatre into a body no less impressionable than the German audience for which he wrote. It was an audience that needed to be jolted into thinking, and smitten hard. (An actor once, rehearsing the part of Azdak in *The Caucasian Chalk Circle*, had the greatest difficulty in coming to terms with this remarkable character. The development of his performance stood still, until the director told him to 'insult the audience' with his acting. The injunction completely transformed his attitude to the part, and his performance flowered from then onwards.) The famous 'Alienation Effect', which the mature Brecht was disinclined to take quite as solemnly as his disciples, means among other things a frankness about the *theatricality* of an honestly interpreted Brechtian performance, and a direct and hard-hitting quality about the monologues and asides to the audience, of which there can be a great many. The actors are conscious of the audience throughout the performance. (Actors are of course always conscious of the audience, but when interpreting Brecht, as opposed to Tchehov, who might be said to stand at the opposite pole as a dramatist, they admit it.) Their acting must be broad and clear, as full of variety and vigour as any acting must be, but technically so presented that it unashamedly seeks its target with a kind of insolent intensity. It is *extrovert* acting that is needed, not the delicate atmospheric drawing in of the audience which is appropriate to Tchehov, and which English actors can do so easily and well. Its opposite they don't do so easily. They are held back by English inhibitions and good manners, and are not used to bludgeoning their equally good-mannered audiences.

The signals to be picked up by any director from a Brecht play can be rewarding for anyone who does not think theatricality to be a pejorative word. But his plays, on English stages, fail more often than they succeed, and it is difficult to avoid the conclusion that not enough thought is given by some directors, *before* starting rehearsals, to the perfectly surmountable problems of interpretation.

The case of Tchehov is different and peculiar. His plays are regularly produced in Britain, in America, and throughout Europe. They have been performed as far apart as South America and Japan. There is not a very great deal about them which is specifically and exclusively Russian: it is their universality which is important. When they are properly acted it seems to matter very little whether the language is Russian, or English, French or German; yet the flavour of Tchehov seems difficult to catch and a bad Russian production of *The Seagull* can be just as bad as a bad English one.

The English are well fitted to do justice by Tchehov—there seems, for one thing, to be a good deal in common between Russian and English humour. And, perhaps because English is not a rigidly precise language, we can take naturally to his *pointilliste* method, which ever rejects the firm outline and gives the Tchehov play an affinity with an Impressionist painting.

Yet it is precisely in this—in the avoidance of the firm outline—that so many productions seem to fail. Actors are trained to be precise and explicit, and most of them at first find it difficult to apply their technique and their training to a kind of acting which may seem vague and diffuse, until it is realized that in its own way it is equally precise and definite. There are other special qualities demanded of Tchehovian performance. In the matter of vocal technique, there must be a refinement and a subtlety which, in spite of complete and easy audibility, presents the illusion of natural conversation, even of intimate thoughts which are barely breathed. (In Moscow they have a way of describing an evening at *The Three Sisters*: they speak of 'visiting them', as if they were actually going to spend an evening with the Prozoroffs.) For the actor whose instinct and training tells him that at all costs he must 'get over', and that the greatest sin he can commit is not to be heard, the hyper-naturalism required seems frighteningly risky. He must, of course, 'get over'. The technical challenge to him is that he must never *seem* to be doing so (although he is in fact projecting his performance into the auditorium just as much as the player of Brecht). The audience must feel that it is being drawn imperceptibly onto the stage: it must be as if they were eavesdropping and becoming part of the very life-blood of these characters' existence. This, of course, is technically difficult, but far less difficult than it seems: it is no more than a refinement of what a trained actor knows perfectly well how to do.

Another essential quality is the unselfish acting and team work which belongs to the best kind of ensemble playing. We pay much lip-service to this in England, and it is the ideal of most actors and directors. But we still see very little of it. It can happen in some of the repertory companies. It can happen at the Royal Shakespeare or the National Theatre, but even

here there is a factor that tends to work against it. In these
illustrious theatres the company is likely to include highly
distinguished players: these may be so used to acting in the
way that stars need to act that they will be unable to subject
themselves to the necessary team discipline.

The problem of accommodating an outsize personality and
an outsize talent into an integrated performance is, in any
event, difficult and complicated. Where Tchehov is concerned,
it becomes almost insuperable. We have as yet no tradition
of ensemble playing in England. When the phenomenon
actually occurs, it strikes the actors as something wonderful
and miraculous (as indeed it is) and not as a normal and
necessary way of doing things, to be taken as a matter of
course. When a star joins a company where the rest of the
actors are on the level of highly skilled non-star ability two
things happen. The company, used to deferring to professional
skill wherever it has achieved deserved prominence, will delay
thinking too deeply about their parts until they get some
idea of what the star is going to do. And the star, though
sincerely co-operative in intention, will think in terms of
expanding the part—which to the star will seem perfectly
reasonable and legitimate. So there is a two-way deterioration
of the ensemble ideal as from the very beginning. As
rehearsals continue, a dominating thought in the company
will be (almost literally) to avoid treading on the star's toes:
they will develop their performances only warily. The star,
taking the opportunity provided by the consequent artistic
vacuum, will expand further into it as if by a natural right.
A point is soon reached when the kind of movement described
on pages 61–62 for the bookcase speech in The Cherry
Orchard becomes unthinkable. If the Liouba is the star she
will almost certainly not tolerate being deprived of the point
of attention which would otherwise come to her exclusively
the moment the bookcase speech begins to lose impact, as it
must. Creativeness becomes stultified because only the star
will have the full freedom to create. Meanwhile the rest of

the company eventually have to do something about their own performances, realizing that if they don't they will make no impression at all. To make some impression then becomes their sole aim. Gone is any idea of balanced team work, of playing the character instead of playing for effect, of the *totality* of the performance. In its place are a number of technicians cleverly yet desperately using their technical skill in competing with each other for a little bit of the limelight.

This of course is an extreme case. Yet I cannot recall a single star production of Tchehov which maintained the true flavour from beginning to end. (An unforgettable level was reached by Rosemary Harris and Laurence Olivier in the Astrov–Yelena scene of the National Theatre production of *Uncle Vanya* in 1964, but the rest of the production was not, in my opinion, of the same standard.) It is interesting that the Tchehov productions which have made the most impact during the past forty years have been *The Three Sisters* of 1938 (with Redgrave and Ashcroft), and the famous Komisarjevsky productions at Barnes twelve years before, with Gielgud, Laughton, and others who later became distinguished. The time to inspire stars with love for team-playing is before they become stars. But circumstances make that particular inspiration fade as they get older and fame comes to them.

Tchehov was possibly one of the first dramatists to take an enigmatic attitude towards the parts he wrote. His first directors, Danchenko and Stanislavsky, received precious little help from him in the elucidation of some of the characters. 'It's all *there*', Tchehov would say, pointing to the script: 'The characters explain themselves.' Nowadays that answer— a very proper one, but one must excuse Danchenko and Stanislavsky, for they were after all faced with something entirely new—has become extremely fashionable. It is to be doubted whether the authors of today really know as much about their creations as Tchehov did. But to explain nothing does at least give the director a degree of freedom greater than he has ever enjoyed before.

With Ionesco, with Pinter, even, it is difficult for the
director to find in the script the kind of hidden backbone
which makes exploration of an inner life in the characters
possible. What the characters are 'really thinking and feeling'
may be anybody's business. There was once a production of
The Birthday Party* in which each of the cast had a different
conception of what the play was about while yet another
conception existed in the mind of the director. But the production was perfectly successful because the sense of tension
which the lines can be made to convey was fully realized.
Pinter's dialogue is filled with opportunities for technical
witchery: the dramatic pause, stretched to imply the uttermost in ultimate implication, the sudden change of pace or
volume, the entire range of theatrical values are there to be
used, without the necessity of linking them to significance.
It would be untrue however to suggest that his plays have no
meaning. Behind what seems disparate and disconnected is the
logic that dreams have. Pinter, himself a first-class actor,
always creates characters who are eminently actable, which
cannot invariably be said of his contemporaries.

The director of much modern drama is free to indulge his
fancy without fear of being meretricious or dishonest. In this
he enjoys a licence sometimes denied to the director of classic
or traditional drama. But he is deprived of one of the greatest
pleasures and responsibilities: he cannot always dig or dip
into the material to solve the question 'Why?' and then help
to supply the answer. He is forced to confine his work to a
level of immediacy and effectiveness. The opportunities he
gets for 'originality' can be no substitute for the denial of
exploration in depth, or of the satisfaction of nursing an
organic growth. He and his actors must be content to deal
only in 'How', comforted and stimulated by the emphasis this
must put on the requisite of technical perfection.

The Theatre of the Absurd and the disparate drama in
general with only the logic of the sub-conscious to give it

* At the Manchester Library Theatre in 1960.

vertebra, is but a moment in the long history of the theatre. The need for some audiences to ask 'Why?' and get some answer, the need for them to seek and find significance in the theatre, and to discover through it a widening of their own experience, must in the long run be satisfied. The values which endure, and those which are merely fashionable should always be kept separate in the mind.

It is ironical and interesting that it should have been Osborne's *Look Back in Anger* that heralded the theatrical revolution of the middle fifties. This play appears to have the values that the revolution itself claims to have toppled over—a story, a good structure (apart from over-writing in various places, which is easily dealt with by the director), well-shaped scenes and characterization in some depth. In fact, it could be called an old-fashioned play. But it gives much freedom to a director to interpret as he chooses. It might seem improbable that Jimmy Porter could ever emerge as a touching character with whom an audience might sympathize because they understand what makes him behave the way he does. Yet this is what happened in a very successful production of the play at the Liverpool Everyman Theatre by Terry Hands in 1965. The director saw it as a tragedy about love and about the pain that lovers can inflict on each other. In doing this he completely transformed the play. He found in the dialogue what he was looking for—and strikingly showed what can come from regarding the script with affection and directing it from a definite and personal point of view.

VII · Production Practice

How does the director actually work in practice? How does he approach rehearsals? What are his relations with his actors, and what is the 'time-table' he uses in piecing a performance together? To answer these questions means considering the way actors work and think, and considering too the different attitudes towards creativity in the theatre in general.

There are many kinds of actors. There are so-called 'technical' actors, there are 'instinctive' actors, there are actors who like to think deeply and all round the problem of bringing their characterizations to life, and there are those who are ill-equipped for thought but who can safely rely on inspiration to show them what they must do. There are lazy actors who never 'get there' till the last moment, and hard-working actors who never achieve more than an unspectacular usefulness however hard they try. The director must be in tune with all of them, and adjust his priorities and his methods of imparting ideas to each individual need.

His first concern with the actor is to discover to which of the two main types he belongs—for his own sympathies are likely to lie with one or the other. (Sympathy is essential: if it is absent a successful relationship with actors is impossible.) The two main types are sharply differentiated: they correspond to two attitudes towards theatre creativity which are fundamentally opposed. There are on the one hand actors who like to think out every possible approach to a play, to a part, to each aspect of a part, well in advance, preparing their interpretation and performance by hard thought and critical

examination of their material. There is a logic in this, but I
do not believe it to be the best way. It leaves something
important out of account, and that is the undoubted power of
such things as intuition and inspiration and sudden feeling
—all 'non-intellectual' elements from which much can be
gained by actor and director, if they will trust themselves to
them, and if they will test them by their critical intelligence
after they have accepted their promptings and not before.

Some of the performers noted for the predominance of
reason and logic in their approach are brilliant and successful.
Yet they often disappoint in actual achievement: they
frequently seem to do less with a great role than is expected
of them. It is in 'pure' comedy that such people come completely into their own and the reasons for this are clear
enough: comedy, as we have seen is an intellectual quantity
and we would therefore expect them to excel at it, because
'humanity' is not involved. When a many-sided exploration
of a human character is demanded of a purely 'intellectual'
actor, he often fails because he is afraid to trust his instincts.
He can always find a good reason for abandoning one 'logical'
interpretation for another which his questing mind tells him
might be better. He tries first this, then that, and never gives
himself to that mysterious creative process that could be his,
since his intellect will never let him admit that the process
exists. Yet exist it undoubtedly does, and directors must
understand how it works. They must know just where reasoning can cease to operate in building up a performance and
where other factors take over. An exclusively 'intellectual'
director, faced with exclusively 'intellectual' actors, will not
achieve much. Their association will be little more than a
battle, to which the victory will go to neither party. The actor
will be unlikely to respond happily to direction and the
director will try to impose his own ideas and will probably
fail. It is a depressing process, and there is no need to describe
it.

The opposite is far more interesting, concerned as it is with the other kind of performer and the other kind of director. Only where intuition is given full play and where the chance of an unexpected flight of inspiration is always present can the creation of a performance by actors and director *together* become an adventure with a happy ending.

Many people imagine that rehearsals should begin with a comprehensive expository lecture by the director to his actors. They think the actors should be given a detailed picture of their characters, clear directions as to the style in which the play is written and full indications of his own intentions and attitude to the script, etcetera. There are indeed directors who actually do this, and their actors have no doubt found the experience extremely interesting. Yet, in fact, a lecture of this kind is quite valueless in its effect on the result, and the director might just as well save his breath. The actor will listen politely: he will attend with genuine interest if the lecture is good enough. But he will listen with that side of himself which has nothing to do with his being an actor; the lecture cannot help him to begin to discover how to play his part, because none of the processes leading to this have yet begun. He will probably discount nearly all that a director says at this stage, and will be groping hopefully yet uncertainly towards a meeting point between himself and the character. The gradual evolution of a performance through three to four weeks' rehearsal is an *organic* process, and nothing can hurry it. The director who does not realize this, and who tries to force the pace by explanations, suggestions and the presentation of ideas, however good, *before* the time is ripe, does not understand actors, and will never be of use to them.

The first ten days of rehearsal are a time of great uncertainty for the actor. The production will suffer not a whit if the director too is 'uncertain' at this stage—that is, uncertain about the same sorts of things as the actor, such as complexities of characterization and motive and the kind of tempi and dynamics with which the character should be expressed.

(As already explained, it is no use his being definite about these things yet: the actor has not reached the point where there is any possibility of him and the director being in tune about them.)

Yet the actor is badly in need of a kind of reassurance in the early stages, and this is precisely what the director can give him, while at the same time laying a firm foundation for the production that is to be built up. The certainty, the firmness, that the director must show is in the practicalities. Such matters as the shape of the set, the positions of doors and windows, chairs and tables, stairs or rostra, are essential points of reference for the performer. They are also the beginnings of what eventually builds up into the atmosphere and general character of the production. These things, being in fact the physical starting point from which the production grows, have to be established firmly in the director's mind and to be expressed equally firmly to the actors at the first rehearsal. The director should work them out accurately in advance, making sure that his designer gives him exactly what he wants. Once rehearsals have started he should not change his mind about them. (There are, unfortunately, well-known directors who remain uncertain about practicalities until even the late stages of their production's growth. If they but knew the dismay they cause to actors by their vacillations! Strangely enough they are often actors turned director, and should know better.)

From the physical fixed points of reference come the beginnings of a creative process. Give King Lear his throne, tell him where stands Cordelia and where stands Gloucester, and he will begin, tentatively, to think of himself as Lear. Tell Gayev in the first Act of *The Cherry Orchard* where his famous bookcase is and let him get used to seeing the other characters on or around their accustomed pieces of furniture and he may find himself playing his imaginary billiards even though his script is still in his hand. From these fixed points the changes of position and the whole pattern of movement of a produc-

tion naturally spring. Moves must be very carefully thought
out and organized, however, and just how the director should
persuade his actors to fulfil the movement-pattern presents
him with what is perhaps his greatest purely practical difficulty.

The difficulty is yet another example of the duality of
theatre. The 'floor pattern' of a production is something that
needs to be assimilated early in rehearsal, for it soon becomes
one of those fixed points of reference which give an actor the
security he needs so much: like the furniture, the doors, the
shape of the set, an actor's characterization can begin to
grow from his moves and positions. But this floor pattern, if
it is to provide a basis on which the entire production can
grow, must be fixed, and in fact arbitrarily fixed. Yet it is also
part of something organic: it must be capable of change.
Moreover, though it is one of the most powerful sources of
atmosphere, of rhythm and expression in any production, it is
composed of a multitude of moves which each actor has to
feel are 'right' both for himself and for the character he is
playing. The pattern cannot therefore be imposed: uncertain
though the performer is of many things at this stage, he is
seldom uncertain about what feels wrong.

The director must project himself into the actor's mind,
and, at the same time, enter imaginatively into the personalities of the characters the actors are playing. If he wants to
be assured of their confidence, he will do this thoroughly
before rehearsals start, imagining the quality and effect of
each move, thus making sure that when he presents it to the
company it will both be the move that he, the director, wants,
and the move the actor will be able easily to accept. (As we
have seen, each move has a dual purpose: it is part of a
character's 'natural' behaviour and expressiveness; and it is
also a means towards the art of pictorial grouping and
rhythmic pattern-making.) On the whole, if the director has
worked the moves out well—done his 'blocking' properly, as
the modern jargon has it—the actors will accept them as

fixed quantities (always with the possibility of change later) and they will gain in confidence by doing so. A director of long experience can safely avoid the tedious slogging of the mental trial-and-error that this preliminary 'blocking' imposes. If he is sure enough of himself, and if the physical features of his set have been evolved with a general idea of the appropriate movement-pattern in mind, he can carry his actors with him while he improvises. But there must be an assurance about this improvisation: he must hit the nail on the head each time. Otherwise his company will be hopelessly bewildered and he will lose their confidence, quite possibly for the duration of the entire production.

During this first period of rehearsals the actor is script-bound. With the book still in his hand, his power of creation is limited, and his imagination, if it leaves the ground at all, seems to do so only in fits and starts. For the director it is a period of watchfulness and assessment. Many ideas may come to him as he listens to the performers reading their lines not particularly well, and sometimes groping for the words in those sections that they are beginning to learn. His problem is to know just when these ideas should be expressed, for unless this happens at the right moment they may well be wasted. The moment must be well judged: it must coincide with the time that the actor's own imagination begins to take flight. And, as atmosphere begins to grow from familiarity with the entrances and exits, as the chairs and tables (mere rehearsal substitutes though they are) begin to acquire a 'cosiness' of personality through being always there day after day, as the moves and positions and sound effects begin to take on reality and conviction, so the actors come nearer and nearer to that time when creativeness really begins. They, if they are wise, have not forced the pace either. They have steadily got on with the drudgery of their scripts with symbols to show where breaths should be taken, where the natural emphases seem to lie, and have made notes on aspects of character suggested by the lines and circumstances.

Until the creative moment comes, what has held it back has been the drudgery of mechanical application. The mechanism of learning lines, the mechanism of making movements, taking up positions which, while there seems nothing 'wrong' about them, have as yet no life of their own: not least of all the mechanism of speaking lines that are either read from a script or incompletely memorized. Suddenly, after a fortnight or so—ten days, perhaps, if the director has urged on the actors the importance of getting the lines learnt, intelligently, not parrot-wise, as soon as possible in order that the drudgery be left behind—the 'moment' comes. The director is able to say to them something like this: 'Let us now behave as if you know your words. You probably don't, but pretend you do. Drink in the "feel" of the scene from each other, take a plunge and "give" yourself to the lines—and let's see what happens!'

What happens at this first attempt is probably very little, but the ice will have been broken: the actors will feel like people who, beginning to learn to swim, for the first time realize that to survive and progress without floundering and sinking is indeed a practical possibility. Now is the time for the director gently yet firmly to make himself felt. In particular it is the time to remind the actors of the inner life behind what they are saying: if they have not forgotten the existence of this they will certainly have lost sight of it in the welter of drudgery and mechanical emphasis which has coloured their work to this point. Now is the time, too, for suggestions about characterization, for from now on the company will be at their most suggestible. It is important to remember over this what are the lines of demarcation between the actor's responsibilities and the director's. It is a mutually accepted obligation that actors and director must agree on what is to be expressed: without agreement on this they should part company, for it is not part of an actor's job to pull against his director about the general objective of the production, which must be in the director's hands. But as to *how* the objective is achieved, in terms of the actor's technical means, this is the actor's responsibility and the director should not attempt to teach him his business.

This rule works, but there are exceptions to it. It applies only to performers of experience and of first-class talent. The director should be able to do an actor's thinking for him, if necessary: but he should do it with tact, never letting the performer feel a sense of inadequacy. This is particularly important when dealing with young actors.

At the beginning of the creative stage of rehearsal the most interesting, as well as the most helpful of the director's contributions, will not be over details: it is in the general slant that can be given that the director's mettle is tested. For example, it is not particularly valuable to tell Gayev in *The Cherry Orchard* either when or how to suck his ju-jubes, or when to play with his imaginary billiard cue, or to remind him that his clothes should be rather elegant and not very new: these things would normally be safely left to him. But what the actor would find stimulating and of practical use (and what in fact is a key piece of direction in any production of *The Cherry Orchard*) would be to be told the following: that Gayev never really completes a sentence and comes to a full stop, because he lives in a world of his own, which has very little to do with his physical surroundings; he comes out of a dream to take part in life when this is forced on his attention, and he relapses into his reveries as soon as his powers of concentration fail him, which they repeatedly do. With such a character, the actor needs to be reminded, there is little room for specific statement, clear definition, and sharply defined beginnings and endings. Such a fundamental piece of direction obviously needs to be given at the first *practical* moment: it will materially affect the characterization of the actor and the whole rhythm of the play. To give it at a later stage would therefore be useless: however good an idea it would seem to be, it would be too late for the actor to make it his own.

There is of course a psychological moment at which all pieces of direction should be given: some are basic to character-development and must be given early; some are more in the nature of embellishments and can be given later. Certain helpful 'slants' can even be given at the last moment, if they do not involve fundamental changes, and if they illumine an aspect of the story or the character which seems to have struck no one before.

Direction should be given in terms of thought or feeling, seldom in terms of a technical objective. The conductor of an orchestra can demand a *pianissimo* without needing to give a reason, but in the theatre the actor cannot be asked merely to take a passage quietly (for the reason that the director 'sees' the moment as a quiet one in the pattern of the whole). The actor needs always to know why he does what he does: 'I think you will find,' therefore suggests the director, 'that the character may want to take this bit softly, for he has probably exhausted his emotional strength in the louder bit he's just done on the previous page.' The actor will almost certainly seize gratefully on the suggestion, untroubled by any thought that the director is manœuvring him into conforming with a part of a plan.

Sometimes it can happen that the director has a new and extremely good idea—but has been inspired too late, when the actor has already built up a solid structure of his part. He then faces the difficulty of convincing the actor that the new way is better than the old. This is by no means always easy to do, since, in the late stage of rehearsal, the actor has so made his performance his own that anything different seems inappropriate, and therefore quite impossible. The director has to use all his reasoning powers here, but to reason is not enough with an actor who by now has got beyond reason and feels he knows by instinct what is right and what is not. Persuasion and tact must be used, together with the promise that if the new way does not work after all, it will be abandoned. A sincere effort to make the change should be asked for, if the director really believes the change worth the effort. For the truth is that actors can in fact make anything 'their own' if they make up their minds to it. This is why some directors are not inclined to be patient with them, realizing that the demands of subjective truth and appropriateness can be over-stated, as exemplified by the claims of American 'Method' actors who put every demand on them through the test of whether they feel 'happy' doing it or not. One must never forget that ever-present duality of the theatre. Most things that the actor does are, when analyzed, 'unnatural', and the test of their suitability is not so simple as merely that it should 'feel right'. Feeling right only has value if it also indicates that a theatrical action will seem true to an audience inside the playhouse in relation to the context. So a director must be prepared firmly to refuse to indulge actors, when indulgence is really all that they are asking for.

We are now, let us assume, well into the creative stage of rehearsals. Ideas have presented themselves thick and fast, and not all of them will have come from the director, who should have no monopoly of suggestions. Indeed, a director who, by creating the right atmosphere at rehearsals, makes it possible for his actors to present ideas of their own, is being just as 'creative' as if he were presenting the ideas himself. Bit by bit the shape of the production forms itself, as the actors seem to 'suck in creativity through the pores of their skins'.* Rehearsals are reaching their climax: a time of great importance, both for director and actors, is at hand.

It is the time when the actors, perhaps tacitly, perhaps not so tacitly, put their director to the test, and either find him wanting or trust him for evermore. It is the time when success is within the director's grasp—but only if he has

* Dame Margot Fonteyn, who in her character-roles has shown herself to be every inch an actress, once spoke of building up her characterization by 'sucking the character in through the pores of her skin'.

earned it by showing his ability to communicate with his
company. It is the moment, in fact, when the production is
about to become finally set in the form it will take at its first
performance: it is the moment when each of the performers
must say to himself 'This is precisely how I am going to play
the part, not that way or the other way, but this way.' For
there are a multitude of ways, it goes without saying, in
which every part can be played, a multitude of ways even
within the bounds of a single general attitude towards the
character as a whole. Any of these ways might be acceptable
to a director and might fall appropriately within his conception of the play. But there is one way that is better than the
rest. It is the way that an actor chooses when he agrees with
a director he respects. It is this that gives him the confidence
he badly needs. On the first night, there is all the difference
between the performance that has this confidence behind it
and the performance which has not. Many actors whose
experience of rehearsals has led them to mistrust their director
will be troubled by doubts, up to the very rise of the first
night curtain, as to exactly how they should deal with certain
specific moments in the play. The effect of such directorial
negligence can be alarming, for the actor tends to panic at
the number of choices still before him. The more intelligent
the actor, the greater his sense of panic is likely to be, for his
talent multiplies the different courses still before him, none
of which seem to be any more obviously worthy of choice
than any other. In the end he chooses because he has to
choose, but he is never fully convinced that the best choice
has been made. Consequently his acting at the first performance lacks ultimate conviction: what might be his best is
only his second best. The director who knows his business
can avoid this situation. He can accumulate such a store of
goodwill, through the way he has handled his actors, that
they will give him their complete trust. Then he can tell each
member of his company to settle for the 'right' course, with
confidence that he will be believed. Actors are easily made

insecure. Once relieved of the burden of choice they can get on with the business of acting.

At the penultimate stage of rehearsals an important check must be made: the director must make sure that his pauses are not too long, and he must be certain to avoid the monotony which happens when performers copy the pace of each other. Both are traps into which it is very easy to fall. An actor can fall in love with pauses. As day succeeds day he can bring himself to believe that by dwelling just a trifle longer—and just a trifle longer again—he has produced more substance. He is wrong. All he has done by his elongation is to indulge his own feelings and to try the patience of his audience. Thought is 'electric' and it uses up surprisingly little time, provided the thought is there. To give an effect more time than it needs is to cheapen it and to sentimentalize it. 'Pace-catching' between actors is the result of laziness (a vice to which the best of performers can sometimes be prone). If actors *listen* properly when rehearsing and playing they will not copy each other's rhythms: but unless they concentrate on listening, and on hearing and speaking lines as if they were hearing and speaking them for the first time in their lives, they will not escape monotony.

Now the production, its timing, rhythm, dynamics, characterization and atmosphere, is very nearly ready. Each element in it, however, needs to come together: the performance needs to work itself in. This can only be achieved by a series of 'run-throughs' in which the actors are allowed to flow through their parts from beginning to end as if they were already performing to the public.

There is a trap for the director here. He is bound always to view his production as a whole; it is its completeness that he is ever working for. He is tempted to try to see that whole too soon, and to demand run-throughs when he still should be working in detail. Actors on the other hand love to work in detail, they can scarcely have too much of it, and they are happy to delay running through until the very last moment

—when it will be too late for the production to leave the ground. A weak director gives himself away if he yields to his actors in this, and does not give himself the chance to see what the production is going to look like. An inexperienced director gives himself away by running through repeatedly. The company then have no chance to ensure that their every moment is filled with consequence and is technically smooth. Run-throughs, however, often give birth to new ideas, and so to the need to work in detail yet again. It is good then to divide the day in two, and to work with a microscopic eye on sections of the play in the morning as a result of notes taken at the run-through on the previous afternoon—and so on.

What, exactly, is meant by 'working in detail'? In every play there are sections which seem to come to life and to become 'real' earlier than others. The actor gets into the habit of linking the gaps between more easily realizable passages by spurious bridges of superficial acting: if he is talented the spuriousness is not immediately apparent. The director has to listen and watch with the sharpest sensibility, to put every line he hears and every action he sees through the most stringent test of credibility. 'What exactly does this *mean*?' he must be constantly asking himself: and it will surprise him to find, if he has had moments of indolence or has failed always fully to concentrate, how often what he has heard turns out to 'mean' absolutely nothing at all. Sometimes the actor is hardly aware that he is being superficial, suffering perhaps only a sub-conscious disquiet here and there. At other times he is acutely conscious that something is wrong, but unless he is given the opportunity—by detailed working—to find out exactly what it is, he will be swept past the troublesome point each day and will face the dress rehearsal with worry in his heart.

In dealing with the director's creative relationships we should not forget his relationship with that most important person, the author. This can bring difficulties. Most directors are on the whole grateful when an author cannot come to rehearsals. This is a pity: but it is the fact. When the director is working on a classic, whose author is no longer of this world, he is certainly relieved of a great deal of worry.

It seems reasonable to think (as many people outside the theatre often think) that the dramatist is the best person to direct rehearsals of his own play. It seems even more reasonable that he should have a great deal to say to the actors about how it should be presented. This belief is however very seldom borne out in practice. Authors are oddly inarticulate when it comes to communicating with actors: they can leave them in a woesomely befogged state just when they themselves feel that they have explained everything to the full. But the difficulty about authors does not cease with the tacit understanding (which has come about since the days of Pinero and Shaw who did successfully direct their own plays) that they must allow their works to be interpreted by others. Authors still have a right to be present at all rehearsals, and it is a right they will never abandon. Nor should they. Yet even their very presence at rehearsals is at best only tolerated, at worst resented by all concerned with putting on the play. This seems unreasonable, yet there is good reason for it. The author, however theatrically experienced, has conceived his play in terms of words and of an ideal interpretation of those words by ideal actors. When he first comes to rehearsal he is immediately subjected to what seems to him a mutilation of his words, by actors who appear not to know what they are doing and who are anyway far from the personalities he had in mind. He is not particularly attuned to appreciate the many things actors and the director will do which have nothing to do with words: he may not even be disposed to think them important. If he is disappointed at what he sees at rehearsal no amount of polite concealment will deceive the actors. If he is not disappointed, the actors will still imagine that he is: he sits at rehearsal, saying not a word, but to the actor he might be thinking anything. It is the inhibiting effect of an author watching him at work that troubles the actor:

the thought that he may be critical prevents him from moving towards making the part his own. Indeed, he can hardly begin that process while the author is there, though he will not mind his presence later—when he has assimiliated the part and it is too late to change his way of playing it. The very opposite is wanted by the dramatist, who not unreasonably feels that it is precisely in the early stages that his presence is essential. The director has a dual role in this situation. He owes it to the dramatist, whom it is his duty to serve, to give him every confidence that he will do his best by the play and will interpret it faithfully. For this he must co-operate willingly with the author and learn all he can from him; he must see, too, that the author is aware of the progress of rehearsals the entire time, and never feels that he is an outsider, deprived of the privileges which are his right. On the other hand he owes it to the company to protect them from any of the embarrassments that the author might cause, and he must tactfully and firmly avoid time-wasting arguments in their presence. It is a delicate, difficult path the director has to follow, and, as in everything else, only experience of many rehearsals and many authors will tell him how best to do it.

At last the production is 'ready': ready, that is, for the confluence of all the work that director and actors have done at rehearsal with the work contributed by other technicians—the scenery, the lighting, the sound effects. We reach the last few hours that remain before the first lighting rehearsal: next comes the dress rehearsal—perhaps, if luck is on everybody's side, a second dress rehearsal—then the curtain must rise on the first performance. It is absurd, but it is at this crucial point when all the elements of performance should blend smoothly, that most productions—all productions in the commercial theatres of the English-speaking world—come up against conditions which put them at risk of being still-born. The painstaking work of an author who may have taken a year to write his play, the concentrated effort of a company of actors who have thought of nothing but the play for a month, the dedicated labour of a director whose mind has been exclusively involved for at least eight weeks, encounter for the first time a lighting technician who has *not* read the play, *not* seen a rehearsal, *not* met the scenic designer, *not* seen a model of the set, and it about to try to operate his lights from a cue sheet for the first time. As if this were not enough, the sound effects will be operating through circuits and loud-speakers which were not used at rehearsal (so that the entire set of volumes of the sound-cues will be different) and the scenic changes, if the production is an elaborate one, will be man-handled by stage-hands who are not only new to the scenery but are quite likely never to have worked in that particular theatre before. It can even happen that when a stage crew has finally mastered its duties at a first dress rehearsal it is reduced to a skeleton at the second dress rehearsal (for English stage-hands today often do two jobs). There can even be occasions when the dress rehearsal crew and the first-night crew are completely different people. The effect of such conditions on highly strung actors is not difficult to imagine. By their own continued hard work they have brought themselves as near perfection as they possibly can. Yet in any English theatre which lacks a large subsidy, economic conditions force them to endure an unrehearsed confusion among the contributory elements—just at the point when they need their support. They cannot be patient in these circumstances; nor, strung up as they are, can the graph of their development continue on the same upward curve that has prevailed throughout rehearsals. The performances in fact go to pieces as the company shrugs its shoulders in the midst of chaos. (Only in the highly subsidized Royal Shakespeare and National Theatres, and perhaps in some of the more fortunate repertory theatres, are there conditions comparable to those of the continental playhouses, where the actors meet the practicalities of staging at least one week before the first performance. But the cost of reform, and our national habit in these matters, make improvement elsewhere unlikely.)

Such conditions naturally demand much patience and control in the director, just when his actors are in danger of losing both. He must concentrate stoically on getting the practicalities right in the short time available, accepting the fact that at this first dress rehearsal his company have given up all thought of 'acting'—or at the very least are giving no more than mechanical performances. This is why he must demand—and get—a second dress rehearsal. At this the actors, conscious that it is their last chance, will begin to give their true performances again. And the technicians (English technicians tend on the whole to be quick in achieving order from chaos) will have become reasonably organized. None the less, when the first night comes no one can be entirely sure what will happen, and this is why first-night nerves are such a dominant element in any first performance.

When the second dress rehearsal is over and the last note has been given, the company should be rested and left unfussed in the few hours remaining before curtain-rise. Foolish is the director who attempts to give any further notes during the first performance itself, or who indeed ventures back-stage at any time after the curtain is up. His work is over. When the curtain comes down, his company will need to be told they have done well, and will want little else. They will be eager for notes the following morning, and each day during the first few days of the run of the play. After that, the director has finished his task. His actors have found a new element to enter into their calculations—the audience. And how they deal with the audience is part of a different story.

F

VIII · 'Personal and Confidential'

'ALL ACTORS incline toward insecurity some of the time, and the best of them much of the time: a director may well be judged by the rapidity with which he can dispel this inclination.'

'What gives actors confidence and ensures that they will give of their best to a director is not the amount or the fluency of his direction but the faith he can inspire that what he says is true.'

'If he frequently visits and comments on a production while it is running the director will do far more than he may realize to keep insecurity at bay. But *at rehearsal* he is not indispensable every single day. He who has the courage to leave actors alone for a day or two will be delighted (though possibly humbled) by the progress and the confidence achieved through a calculated absence.'

'In handling actors, the Great Boyg's instruction to Peer Gynt "to go the long way round" should be remembered. By obeying this, that vulnerable source of the actor's creative power, his ego, is preserved from a possibly fatal puncture.'

'A director may change his mind as often as anyone else, but he must foresee the moment beyond which a change of mind will be fatal.'

'Inaudible actors are not to be borne, but actors who shout are intolerable. The director should never say 'louder' or 'softer' to actors: if he does he will merely exchange one bad thing for another. He must speak always in terms of what is artistically true and of what is intelligible to the audience.'

'Many matters that seem "wrong" about production and acting will right themselves before the dress rehearsal without the director having to do much about them. But only experience can warn a director which are those things which should be left alone, and which are those that must be dealt with in good time if there is not to be a fatality.'

'Everything the director does is for the ultimate benefit of the audience: consequently a performance played *downstage* as near to the audience as possible is immeasurably more compelling in its effect than the same performance played six feet further *upstage*.'

'If a director can find for two actors the right relative positions in which to play a dialogue he can reach what no amount of psychological illumination can achieve: in the correct positions the actors, surprisingly, will illuminate themselves.'

'Physical vitality is one of the director's most precious assets. Without this, his knowledge and his understanding may well fail to make themselves felt. A tired director lets small inadequacies go by, without summoning the energy needed to interrupt. A bad production is often no more than a succession of small inadequacies: thus the director may exhaust his actors but must never exhaust himself first.'

These are all simple and obvious statements: there is nothing in them that has not more than once been said before. But the assertions are true; they 'work'. Many a director has suffered regrets and many a production has been fatally marred because some of them have been ignored. They make an appropriate opening to what is a partly personal last chapter, because I arrived at their truth not by sensible deduction as might be imagined, nor by seeing them in print, but only by practical and painful discovery.

Few people have managed to teach me anything, and these few I mention now with enduring gratitude. My first sight of theatre wisdom was due to a director who was not concerned with teaching but only with getting a tolerable result from some ill-assorted material of which I was a part. Theodore Komisarjevsky had agreed to direct *King Lear* for the Oxford University Dramatic Society. (Theodore Komisarjevsky, whose sister Vera was the first Nina in *The Seagull* and a very famous actress in old Russia, was responsible in great measure for the renaissance in English acting which took place from the mid-twenties to the mid-thirties.) Six weeks of rehearsal under him (and another six weeks a year later when he unaccountably undertook a second production for the O.U.D.S.) filled me with a firm faith in the effectiveness of the oblique directorial approach. Komisarjevsky 'did' nothing with his collection of scholars, besotted afficionados and earnest would-be actors, yet somehow he made it possible for each of them to give the best of which they were capable. Afterwards, few of them ever realized how the trick was done. Part of the trick was due to his never bruising a single aspiring ego, but on the contrary, to his encouragement for all to spread themselves, as he seized and built upon what he needed for his purpose, while quietly deflecting elsewhere the grosser crudities of those ever-confident amateurs. The rest of it came, of course, out of very great knowledge and very great patience. The result was a *King Lear* which is remembered by some even today.

The lesson of 'Komis' was vividly reinforced in my first professional engagement when I played a small part and was Assistant Stage Manager in a pair of Spanish plays at The Royal Court Theatre in 1928. The plays had been adapted by Harley Granville-Barker, and Barker, on behalf of the authors, was to be present at all the rehearsals. At the end of the first day's work it became clear that the abilities of the director were not up to the standards of the distinguished adaptor, and through a substitution as swift as it was ruthless the director obligingly vanished (though his name was retained on the bills) while Barker took over his duties. I, an A.S.M. and would-be director of twenty-three, was suddenly privileged to observe the work of the most illustrious director of British stage history.

It is a fallacy that stage managers can learn much about directing by watching their superiors—stage managers have to work too hard at their own duties for that. Many priceless crumbs of knowledge dropped all about me and I missed most of them. But I could hardly avoid noting Barker's outstanding mind, the total grasp of his subject, the immense range of his abilities and the fiery intensity of his concentration, which seemed almost fanatical. Neither could I fail to note that he was no Komisarjevsky. He invariably went straight to the point, explaining with penetrating clarity what he wanted an actor to do and how he should do it. If he could not get what he wanted, however, he would persist in pressing on with his attempt, with a relentless and unflagging energy which left the actor utterly exhausted. Sometimes it was obvious to everyone present except Barker that his objective, in its original and unmodified form, was unattainable; nevertheless his mode of attack never varied. The sufferer in this particular production was John Gielgud, who was cast to play a sturdy and extrovert young Spanish peasant and who, in consequence, was expected to belie his personality, his nature, and his physique. Barker worked like a demon for the 'truth' of the part, but when it became clear that this, in its most obvious sense, was not available, he turned his back on that other and equally valid 'truth' which is discoverable not in externals but in the creative being of a perceptive artist. I wondered whether Barker, with his almost obsessive single mindedness of approach, had any inkling at that time of the range of sensibilities which Gielgud had already shown in other plays. And all my youthful instincts rose in rebellion, seeming to tell me that Barker's way, for all its brilliant intellectuality, led not towards creative acting but towards suffocation.

I resolved to follow the 'fluid' example of Komisarjevsky,

and since I knew nothing then about the theatre's duality I did not realize that a director needed to be both fluid and rigid at the same time. This led me soon to do work which was undisciplined and sloppy (I obtained enough work to earn my living, though it was poorly paid: in those days a director in his early twenties was virtually unique, and my scarcity value brought me offers, though sometimes very undistinguished ones). Thus, my path was neither easy nor wisely charted.

I learned some valuable things on the way, however; some of them from playwrights. Lionel Hale* it was who first made me aware of the importance of movement in theatre. He showed me, albeit he was a writer and even younger and less experienced than I, how sometimes the appropriate 'choreography' would enhance the value of a line, however good that line might be. Another playwright, Michael Egan,† taught me that all stage dialogue, however unassuming, needs to be rehearsed and conducted like music, that it must never stay for long on one note but must go up and down in pitch and volume and vary in tempo at all times. At rehearsals, whenever his dialogue seemed to him to become boring—as the result of my neglect of these important matters—this author would rapidly rotate his arms like windmills, to show his irritation. And it was C. K. Munro‡ who demonstrated

---

* Lionel Hale wrote a number of witty and fanciful comedies in the early thirties, and I was fortunate enough to direct three of them. Later he became the feared critic of the *News Chronicle*, and was the only critic of the time really respected by actors. Later still the B.B.C. claimed most of his time, to the theatre's great loss.

† The author of *The Dominant Sex*, a social comedy owing much to the plays of Ibsen, which I directed and which ran for nearly two years in the middle thirties. His subsequent plays unfortunately were not so successful.

‡ C. K. Macmullen, a civil servant who under this pseudonym made a sizeable reputation in the middle twenties with a political expressionist drama called *The Rumour*. This was produced all over Europe. It was later followed by the highly successful 'commercial' comedy *At Mrs Beam's*. I directed a much later play of his, which was seen by very few people.

to me the fundamental principles of economy, clarity and timing in all stage business, and particularly in all that appertained to comedy. A commercial theatre manager,* even —a most respected one in his day—taught me something of the greatest importance: this was to keep my actors *down stage* so as to prevent them dissipating their powers in performing behind the furniture. 'Don't bury your artists, are you ashamed of them?' he once whispered into my reddening ears in the middle of a rehearsal—and the whisper could be heard throughout the entire theatre. A shock delivered by Lewis Casson gave me a valuable lesson in humility. I met him in a railway carriage at a time when I was already quite well established and I complained to him bitterly of the young director's lot, since almost invariably the material available to him, and which earned him his bread-and-butter was unworthy of his respect. Sir Lewis' answer was blunt and to the point: if I could not respect what I was doing I had better stop doing it.

The reader may well find it odd that I had to find all these things out in the way I did; that apparently I had thought none of them out for myself. But unfortunately I suffered much from mental laziness, and I cannot say that I deserved what early success I managed to achieve.

In my beginnings what excited me most about theatre was the variety and the subtlety of the moods it could express. The possibilities—of harmony, and dissonance and counterpoint, and of the thrilling exploration of the mystery of the timing of speech—seemed endless. It was enough for me that these possibilities existed to be made apparent by a sensitive director, and it was of course not a little gratifying that the signals in the script of this play or that, which seemed to me

---

* Horace Watson, who owned and managed the Theatre Royal, Haymarket, for many years (in the U.S.A. he would be styled a 'Producer'). The play I directed for him was *Supply and Demand* by Aimée and Philip Stuart. This was my first West End production, and a failure.

to be so clear and unmistakable, were often missed by my rivals. These directors could not have been very receptive, I thought.

The reasons for the moods in which I so delighted did not in those early days spring powerfully to my mind: I was more occupied in feeling about a script than in taking each element of it to pieces and thinking about it. And I lacked the capacity to concentrate. I had, however, an immediate grasp of the 'feel' of a play and to some extent a natural instinct of how to approach it. This allowed me to seem attractive and interesting in my first contacts with authors and with managements and actors; thus the start of each engagement appeared most propitious to all concerned. Rehearsals, however, too often proceeded on uninteresting lines and I was often less popular by the time the play reached performance. The pattern of my career was thus too frequently a series of hopeful beginnings and rather dis-appointing endings. Part of my trouble sprang from the mental laziness I have already mentioned, but a great deal of it came from an inherent fear of actors, which afflicted me for a great many of my early years. I was not a good actor myself (though here again I had many of the right instincts) and I had never been formally and technically trained. This gave me a great respect for actors, but respect of the wrong kind. I admired them without understanding them. My lines of communication with them were poor and if I failed to establish my influence with a cast at the start I would often fail to achieve that flexible yet clear-cut control which was so very necessary. The actors, in turn, must have been baffled by me. My directions to them were rather like the 'happenings' of today: they had no cause, other than that of a so-called inspiration, no history beyond the fact that the rehearsal on the previous day showed gaps which needed to be filled by something. If the script happened to be a comedy I would sometimes think of funny things for the actors to do—be-cause comedy interested me and has always done so. I can well remember the looks on the faces of some of my casts at those times: sometimes they looked puzzled, sometimes resigned. Occasionally they would look surprised and not displeased as, every now and then a comedic effect actually occurred as the result of carrying out my directions. But more often than not a funny idea of mine would turn out to be as theatrically compelling as a heap of hardening concrete, and the effort, which was nearly always carried out with astonishing conscientiousness on the part of the actor, would have to be abandoned.

Then, one day, one of my leading actresses happened to be Athene Seyler, and when I suggested that it would be amusing if she performed a certain evolution she simply said 'Why?'

I did not know.

It seemed to me that if I could possibly avoid the repetition of that experience I should do so.

I came at last, through painful steps, to realize something that ought to have been clear to me a long time before—simply that all events in the theatre are inter-connected, that everything a performer does must have a reason rooted in truth, and that this truth is of many kinds, and usually (though not always) based on human character. (The qualification is important, for it brings within the principle such apparently aberrant characters as those in *The Importance of Being Earnest*, with many other people of comedy, and even allows us to include those artefacts who populate the plays of Ionesco and the Theatre of the Absurd, where the Law is the logic and the attitude of the author himself.)

From Athene Seyler I learnt the inescapable fact of the theatre's duality and many other things, not the least of which was that to express the truth of an emotion is not the same thing as to give a true expression of it whenever it crops up. Merely to express an emotion, though it is obviously better to do so truthfully than falsely, is still only to act from the *outside* and to leave the heart of the matter out of account.

F*

To make an audience experience the truth of a feeling one must relate the feeling to the context, and show the reason for it, as well as the true feeling itself, inside a fully rounded character: only if he does this does the performer really act in depth.

Thus, through this single experience with a powerful comedienne, who in her younger days was also an emotional actress of rare delicacy, I began an education in understanding the *genus actor*. And I always continued to be fascinated by the way in which the elemental nursery instinct to make believe can become transformed in a very few individuals to a skill demanding a consummate discipline and control.

The path I took at the time of the encounter with Athene Seyler was partly the result of choice, and partly a matter of taste and personal predilection. I could have answered her embarrassing question with a 'that's how I want it', and some directors would undoubtedly have reacted in that way. I was, however, too young at that time to do any such thing. As I look back I note that it would be pleasant to think that it was not entirely timidity but an instinct for the right values which made me suddenly see that moment of the play from the actress's point of view. Certainly the latter formed part of the truth, if not the whole of it. In any case, I realized at that time that I must always look at a production with the actor's eyes as well as with my own.*

In this conclusion I was involved with yet another example

---

* This does not mean that a director should give in to actors each time they present a good case for having their own way. When Judith Anderson played Arkadina at the Old Vic in the centenary production of *The Seagull* she did not want to play the scene discussed on page 47 in the manner explained thereon. It was important to me that the values I saw in that particular moment should be expressed, yet nothing would have been worse than if the actress had essayed the scene unwillingly with bad grace. Equally, a flat refusal to accept direction would have prejudiced the entire production. In the event, a sincere effort on her part to give the effect a trial resulted in Judith Anderson's complete acceptance of the idea *with her mind*, and the 'problem' was solved.

of the theatre duality. 'Duality', I soon realized, however, could not mean any escape from responsibility. A director cannot trust to luck and hope that failure to do well by one side of the picture can be remedied by success in a different aspect of it: every department requires exactitude and a fair measuring out of the emphasis due to each of the balancing elements. To look at a growing production and a developing characterization *solely* with regard to what the actor feels is best for himself is fraught with danger, and encourages the endemic vices of the actor.

Laissez-faire of this kind misleads, in particular, the young, actor as he climbs the painful incline towards achievement. His path is difficult enough. It is beset by irrelevancies, not the least of which is the importance given nowadays to the external trappings of theatre instead of to what really matters. Theatre technocracy is in danger of becoming intoxicated with its own power. Experts on acoustics, experts on this kind of stage and that kind of stage, experts on lighting, experts on every aspect of theatre design—these have sprung up round us in the last decade like toadstools.

In all this the actor himself is sometimes forgotten, as well as the fact that the only things which really determine the theatrical quality of a nation are its dramatists and the quality with which these are interpreted.*

I am concerned, naturally, not with the 'personality' who hopes for a fortune in films and television, not with the hanger-on of show-business who sells his meagre talents to anyone who will buy them for a limited period. It is the vocational actor who is always in my mind. For him the theatre's duality extends to the very core of his being. Within

---

* To quote an example near home. The Nottingham Playhouse in the latter part of the fifties, reached the highest standard of acting and direction under its director Val May that in the writer's opinion was ever attained by any repertory theatre in the country during that decade. This standard has not always been reached again since the sleazy little converted cinema-house was replaced by one of the finest and most modern theatres in provincial England.

him can co-exist the seeds of the uttermost egotism and self-indulgence, together with those of an obsessive and puritanical devotion to the demands of his art. In a balanced synthesis of typical attributes he can be a matchless servant of the community. To this he should strive, however much he may fall short as inevitably he must. To act is to *give*: it is not to indulge, it is not to exploit; the actor literally gives himself to his audience. He confers upon them an extended vision of life, expressing its essence as first seen by a writer, and planting this firmly in their consciousness. He does this by his talent, his imagination and his technique.

Much controversy springs from this belief, rooted partly in ignorance and partly in muddled thinking, that technique and imagination are opposing concepts and that to emphasize the first is to atrophy the second. Nothing, however, could be farther from the truth. The Greek word for art and the Greek word for technique are one and the same. A ballet dancer's spine of steel enables him to appear feather-light, but he has created that spine out of years of patient toil at the dreariest of technical exercises. So, too, an actor's upholding technique has permitted him to float freely on the wings of his imagination, and to do so night after night without blurring the sharp focus of his performance. There are, inevitably, actors who are mere clever-dicks and whose lack of imagination is compensated for by technical agility: these can perform a confidence trick upon their public and their success is a kind of sleight-of-hand. The sterility of the performances of those actors itself indicates that technique without imagination just will not do, but it also gives encouragement to the view, widely held during the period of 'Method' predominance in America, that technique is unnecessary and even destructive. This view is not entirely dead even today, yet the belief collapses whenever theoretical discussion is replaced by actual practice.

For illustration there is the parable (like all parables allegedly based on truth) of the eager young American performer who was instructed by a 'Method' director to 'forget he was in a theatre' while playing the small part of a postman. American theatre discipline at that time permitted him to run down the street outside the stage door 'delivering letters', timing his arrival on the set so that he would appear on his cue and at the same time be in tune with the psychological demands of his part. Unfortunately he had left the audience out of his calculations, and on one particular night these elected to laugh louder and longer than usual at the line which happened to be his cue (his brother actors having found out by actual experience that this was a comedy line) with the result that his well-meaning intentions were ruined. He was forced to wait in the wings, as no real postman would, until the laugh was over. The damage done to the young man's half-baked conceptions of what was really needed from him is not on record.

The responsibility which comes from a duality which is fundamental simply cannot be evaded. However deeply an actor may feel his character he still has to express it in terms of a voice which is limited in part by nature and in part by what he has done to train it, and in terms of bodily movements which answer more perfectly or less so to orders from his brain. And whatever the degree of the actor's feelings he must still implant those in the hearts of an audience which has paid, nowadays rather heavily, to see him. How then, should the novice actor proceed at the threshold of his career, in order to be fit to serve his fellow men? There are so many 'disciplines' and 'techniques' demanding his submission and his competence. But, nevertheless, there are priorities. The first priority for the young actor is to avoid a hardening of opinion about philosophies of acting, to avoid becoming a disciple of any philosophy, before he has found for himself a firm and unassailable technique. The second priority is a determination to work hard and long to learn that technique. Only when he has achieved the latter and the professional confidence which comes with it will he find that there are still many questions to which he will want to find the answers, and in finding these he is very likely to discover his own philosophy of acting. He will find, too, (if he has avoided a slavish dependence on any pedagogue) that Stanislavsky has said a great many things which he had always known in his heart to be true, but which he had never before seen so well expressed in black and white.*

However, for a young actor to steep himself in Stanislavsky before he has learnt the basic elements of his craft and some maturity as a person, is to run into a morass. Consider:

> . . . the more an actor tries to entertain the spectator, the more will the spectator sit back like a lord, and wait to be entertained, without making the slightest effort to take part in the creative work that is taking place before him; *but as soon as the actor stops paying any attention to him, the spectator will begin to show an interest in him, especially if the actor is interested in something on the stage* [the italics are mine] *that the audience, too, finds important.*†

There is truth in this, but there is great danger in an inexperienced or untrained actor taking such a passage literally, especially the sentence in italics. That a novice would feel encouraged, because it is so much easier, to develop the habits of fussy 'business' and disregard of the audience that have made the 'Method' so notorious is all but inevitable: and such, of course, is the very opposite of what Stanislavsky was trying to achieve.

I found it very necessary, in my own history, soon to come to terms with Stanislavsky, to try to discover what he was and what he was not. His writings were no inspiration to me as a director, for it seemed to me, and still seems to me, that

* For some best actors in depth, however, Stanislavsky is anathema, since he says what they would rather leave unsaid, this in their opinion causing self-consciousness to stifle inspiration.

† *Building a Character* by Constantin Stanislavsky, translated by Elizabeth Reynolds Hapgood, Reinhardt, London, 1950.

he was not a very good one.* He was an amateur who became, partly through intelligence and partly through experience, a very good actor; as such he had to dig out for himself the clay of commonplace professional necessity as well as the gold of professional creative means. He dug from the unpromising soil of a Russian Theatre which was congealed in conservatism and self-satisfaction. He sluiced away the dross with his powers of imagination, though these were not without their limits, as can be seen from some of his ideas on the direction of Tchehov's plays. His prose can be embarrassing in its English translation and, on occasion, it can be 'obscure': his reasoning is often tortuous and his arguments repetitive. It is easy to miss the point of the dull sections, yet these often contain some of his best thinking. A novice, on the other hand, is likely to be most impressed by those paragraphs which, like the one just quoted, can be most glibly interpreted to mean what he would like them to mean. All untrained actors would like nothing better than to forget that anybody is watching them, and in passages such as this Stanislavsky appears to give his blessing to a repudiation of the actor's duty to compel the attention of the audience that has paid to watch him.

No, Stanislavsky is no help to the beginner. How, then, can the beginner begin to solve the obvious dilemma of the theatre's duality? The answer I have met—which must have been met by many others who have tried to help actors—is an obvious answer. It is simply that matters of technique, and matters of feeling and thought, must be studied *together*, and the problems raised solved together. There can be no solution as to the perfect way to deliver a line with rhythm, clarity and beauty of tone, unless there is a complete exploration and understanding of the *feeling* to which the line owes its existence. On the other hand, the un-technical actor who, as he thinks, is expressing the most passionately 'real' emotion is in fact doing nothing of the kind: if he does not know how to

* See pages 108, 109.

employ the means appropriate to the feeling the audience will
not receive what he imagines he has transmitted to them. All
they then get is a distorted, blurred or otherwise imperfect
version of the emotion or thought he intended them to have.
Recognition of duality in fact leads towards the solution of the
problems it raises, for the feeling will always point the way
towards the appropriate means. But to deny the means is
merely inevitably to lead back to the cul-de-sac of the Method.
Stanislavsky wrote this: *

> There does exist, however, another *natural* [my italics]
> musical resonant form of speech which we note in great
> actors in moments of genuine artistic inspiration.
>
> An actor must acquire this musical speech for himself
> *by exercising his voice under the control of his sense of
> truth* [my italics] almost to the same degree as a singer
> does. . . . .
>
> An actor interpreting a part in terms of his own
> understanding of it will not forget that each sound
> which forms a word, each vowel as well as each
> consonant, is a *separate note* which takes its place in the
> tonal chord of a word: it expresses this or that small part
> of the soul of the character that filters through the word.

In that is the gold of Stanislavsky. Nowhere have the
fundamentals of the actor's art been better expressed. The
exercise of the voice under the control of a sense of truth is
precisely what a student actor does when he is being properly
trained. In order to do it he has first developed vocal power
by exercising his diaphragm and the means of controlling his
breath, and has gone on to perfect his control by acquiring
flexibility in his rib muscles and the muscles of his lips and
tongue, attaining complete mastery of his body through the
ability to relax his throat, neck and each separate limb.
It was the realization of this degree of mastery over physical

* *Stanislavsky's Legacy*, edited and translated by Elizabeth Reynolds
Hapgood, Reinhardt, London, 1959.

self that brought me inevitably to my present respect and
affection for good actors and all of their kind. Yet it was a
long time before I came either to know or to understand them
enough, and consequently before I came to know as much as
I should about the tools of my own trade.

I once did a play in which Peggy Ashcroft played the part
of a suburban housewife. At the second rehearsal she wanted
to make her first entrance carrying a tray. She needed to
know, very properly, exactly why she was coming into her
own living room. I had considered the tray a cliché and had
deliberately avoided it, thinking that she ought to have been
able to think of a 'more imaginative' way of coming onto the
stage for the first time. She felt that this 'more imaginative'
entrance should come from me: meanwhile she continued to
bring on the tray. She got her way, since I could think of
nothing better. In this she was not unreasonable. What she
needed, I now realize, was to feel *secure* at this first entrance:
the tray may have been a cliché, but it was *right*; it made her
feel she belonged in her own home and freed her mind from
such elementary details so that she could concentrate on the
things about her part that mattered.

The need to feel secure is deeply important to actors, but I
had forgotten that even the illustrious and the vastly experienced can be bewildered as children if their security is in the
least menaced. That is why many stars wish to be 'directed'
by a weak director—a man who will neither inspire their
performances nor force them unwillingly to form part of a
grand design, but who can be relied upon, on the other hand,
to ensure exactly the physical conditions under which they
feel they can act best.

A *basic* security is, of course, what an actor's technique
brings him. Such security is what enabled Edmund Kean to
count the number of steps he took before reaching that part
of the stage where he was to speak a certain line, and to do
so without losing either truth or passion. Such it was that
permitted Talma to say 'Angels and ministers of grace defend

us' from off stage, and to chill his audience to the marrow despite the fact that he spoke Shakespeare's lines in the middle of a funny story that he was telling to someone who was waiting in the wings. Such faith in technique it was that made the great Salvini say : 'an actor lives, weeps and laughs upon the stage, and, while weeping or laughing he *observes* [my italics] his laughter and his tears'. But these performers of a past age were none of them menaced by the games of a cynical director or by the unimaginativeness of a stupid one. If Peggy Ashcroft, with all her technique at her disposal, could be made apprehensive by my own want of sensitiveness, the plight of the inexperienced actor in the hands of a director who is not interested in acting can be imagined. The beginner in the profession is in any case deserving of sympathy, for he longs for a kind of help which he almost never gets. This is the help that he might reasonably be expected to obtain from his seniors, and which the continental theatre with its many long-standing permanent companies and its tradition of paternalism is accustomed to provide. The continental actor feels a certain responsibility for those who follow in his footsteps and the older and more distinguished he is the more likely is he to show this by devoting some of his spare time to practical work with dramatic classes or private pupils. Such is not the custom in the English-speaking countries, and the deficiency points an accusing finger at some of our older actors (the younger ones are far more generous and very much more ready to help each other). I do not remember any instances where an actor over middle age has taken the trouble to tell a beginner how he might improve his performance (though, occasionally, I have known an elderly actress give advice to a young girl). But instances of complaint, of unkindness, of impatience on the part of the well-practised towards the inexperienced can hardly be missed by those who observe actors for any length of time. I have found this aspect of the profession most disagreeable. The fact of it has made me infinitely prefer, with a few exceptions, the younger actors to the older ones.

My preference for the young was possibly a factor in my being offered the Principalship of the Royal Academy of Dramatic Art—an offer which otherwise might well seem unaccountable. My acceptance of the post, though it led to my bringing in younger acting instructors and, through these, to many much-needed reforms for that institution, led also very naturally to an open declaration of where my sympathies lay. The majority of the Council of the Academy was composed of elderly actors and actresses and their associates. Sybil Thorndike, Flora Robson, Athene Seyler and the late Diana Wynyard were conspicuously interested in all developments of the curriculum and in the plans that were being made for the future. Peter Daubeny, too, was an enthusiastic and helpful critic. The activity of these, however, did not compensate for the apathy of the rest, and it was quite impossible for me to forgive this dreary majority for their total lack of interest in the students for whom they were, nominally at least, responsible. They, of course, quite naturally could not forgive me for finding their indifference so deplorable. The result of the clash between us is now ancient history.

A young actor, then, has no one to help him and no insurance against failure except a faultless technique. Once he has attained the confidence of a Talma so that he may watch his own performance without either being shocked by it or falling in love with it, he may safely set out, if he feels the need, on such speculative paths as were explored by Stanislavsky. And if he does so he may profit.

'The Masters that direct the actor's powers,' said Stanislavsky, 'are Feeling, Mind and Will.' The young actor's feeling is not in doubt: this has been with him ever since he began to dream of acting. His mind, during his training, must discipline his feeling, always relating it to the character to be explored, and actually directing the process of exploration. His Will, however, is something else, something which will determine just how valuable (however 'good' they are) the other 'Masters' will be allowed to become. Without the strength of a strong will, neither feeling, nor mind, will be of any use.

It is not merely the obvious fact that a determined will is essential to a purposeful career. It is not merely that strength of will can ensure that a career is aesthetically economical and tidy, uncluttered by irrelevancies and unthreatened by any unconscious deterioration of personal standards. The will to concentrate on the *vitality of truth* is essential during creative rehearsals and during actual performances. Failure in this respect is characterized by the prevailing sin of the inadequate professional, which is not that his emotion is *false* (for false acting has very nearly disappeared today) but that it is *feeble*. 'True' emotion, which cannot rise in its context to the appropriate intensity, is just as bad and just as 'false' as the emotion which is false in the first place. Yet the avoidance of this feebleness of effect presents quite a difficult problem and the better the actors under the director's command the more difficult the problem becomes.

I can remember saying to Celia Johnson in 1932, to Flora Robson in 1956, and to members of my present company in Michigan in 1967: 'What you are doing is *absolutely right*; but just give me *more* of it, deeper, more intensely felt feeling, more vivid responses'. Yet actors, if they are good, are usually baffled by such an injunction. They are afraid of the falsification caused by over-acting, and when they are at the point at which the director says such things they are usually also at the point—or they think they are—when they know very well that any purely technical intensification will achieve nothing. It is an *inner* intensity that they need, and this is arrived at only by a degree of concentration very difficult to reach except by a gradual process in rehearsal after rehearsal. It cannot be forced.

To a certain extent it can be achieved by training. Vladek Sheybal used a Stanislavskian exercise at R.A.D.A. for the purpose. The students would sit facing each other very closely and looking into each other's eyes. Each opposing partner would then pour out a stream of improvised and self-assertive dialogue with the intention of maintaining both the sense and the force of his own words so that his 'meaning' could prevail over that of his opponent. Whoever lost the contest by failing to out-concentrate the other was silenced. The exercise developed the will of each individual, encouraging his ability to centre on a feeling and to keep it strong and true, no matter how great the distraction. No one who succeeded in this competition would ever after fail in attack or power of emotion.

A corollary to the exercise was used, of course, for 'duality' made this necessary and imaginative inspiration could not be neglected at the Academy. Here the student regarded his opposite number intently, trying to divine what lay behind his eyes, and letting himself express whatever thoughts occurred to him as the result of his awareness of another human being. The uninventive student would simply copy the expression of his partner in the exercise: the imaginative one would extend his own activity as the completion of a pattern begun by the other. The exercise was, of course, wordless, and it did much to stimulate inventiveness. More than that it extended the boundaries within which empathy could operate unfettered and so helped young actors to be good at ensemble playing.

All my experience with actors of all kinds, and all my experience with dramatic students, has led me to detest the thought of ever treating them like puppets, as certain directors like to do. But despite this, I have spent too much of my life using them without analyzing their processes. The director who does not understand the actors who work under him forfeits, if he only knew it, all influence in that quarter where the most important part of his work is done. It has taken me many years to realize this, and one of the consequences of that realization is the knowledge that no book about direction is complete if it does not include an indication of how a performer thinks. The following notes were set down by a young professional who was once asked to discuss the 'actor's creative processes' before, during rehearsals and at actual performance.*

BEFORE REHEARSAL

(1) Read play.

(2) Read play analytically, asking self questions: what play is about, time, place, circumstances; who are they; what are their relationships with each other. Try to see each of the important characters from his own point of view and from the point of view of the others.

(3) Own character: get all possible information from script: past life, relations with others, physical and mental characteristics, aims for self: what others say about my character, what are my character's self revelations and statements *and see if and how these things differ from each other.* [My italics].

(4) Define character's basic motivation(s). These are often so obvious that I completely overlook them at first. I recently played someone whose sole activity was to order other people about. It was weeks before I discovered that the character did this in order to feel on a par with the others, and, really because of a feeling of inferiority to the others. This is such a cliché that I completely ignored it at first, but not until I grasped it and accepted it could I begin to play the part from the 'inside out'.

(5) Get from script important incidents from past life and imagine them fully, improvising or writing down details, if it helps.

(6) Work on script, mainly on own scenes, but keeping track of others. Try to work out my motivations and those of others important to me. All this will grow in rehearsal of course, but it helps me to rough it over first, to start living with the character.

* British Actors Equity Membership Card Number B 14484.

(7) Study shapes of my scenes, see how I think they should be played *as scenes.*

(8) Imagine in detail anything complicated or important that I have to describe or see in the mind's eye. Especially if it is something that I am supposed to know well. Then I imagine it over and over again until I'm really familiar with it, putting in fresh details from time to time to keep it alive.

(9) Emotion Memory (Stanislavsky's term) and Sensation Memory—the basis of acting, I think. Once I can bring into a play a really vivid memory of a feeling towards a person, place or object; or once I can bring to it a physical sensation, my imagination begins to work and to adjust that feeling, until it stops being part of my own private life and becomes part of the character's relationship with someone else, or part of his reaction to a place or an object. This change may not happen until late in rehearsal. Sometimes, I find, it never happens at all. Until it does, I have constantly to remind myself of the real (my own) memory and keep all the circumstances of this fresh in my mind.

The insight into acting which this gives to a director is without price. Noteworthy is the degree of concentrative effort which the performer demands of himself, and also the fact that an actor may be posing precisely those questions which a director should be asking, and to which a good director should be able to find the answers. This performer shows, too, an awareness of those very values which the director should be accustomed to regard as being within his own province.

Paragraph 4 is significant. The performer accepts the blame for missing 'the obvious'. Yet the director concerned apparently missed it too, with far less justification. Paragraph 5 shows that the imaginative process only begins after a great mass of 'facts' about the character have been painfully dug out. This is most important in considering the ordering of rehearsals and just at what moment the actor should be given ideas and suggestions.* The key word is 'fully'. Many people think they are perfectly capable of 'imagining' fictional events or events they have read in newspapers. In fact they do no more than to allow the images the writer has invented to float before their mind's eye like a cinema film. Such people receive these pictures for nothing, having had to do no work in order to see them: consequently what they 'see' lacks any sort of vividness or permanence: it is quickly forgotten. To the actor, imagining is quite a different process: he must actively *seek* the images, and sometimes the pictures he conjures up for himself are far more powerful than anything the words of the part might seem to suggest. Only by long and patient concentration in undisturbed seclusion can the needed intensity of imagination be found, felt, and recorded in the actor's memory.

Improvisation is mentioned. This is a term which often crops up when methods of training actors are discussed, and much useless activity and even harm can be done in its name. It is a convenient umbrella under which the untalented acting teacher can very easily acquire a spurious reputation for being clever. (Mere charades can result when an acting teacher sits back and tells a class to improvise, particularly as such activity is likely to include the obligation to provide dialogue. The demand that illustrative words be found by young actors who, if they know how to spin the right words would have chosen another vocation, is extremely destructive. It can quickly build up inhibition and tension and stifle the capacity to 'improvise' altogether.) But improvisation for a specific practical purpose, as when a performer works on a part in private, is another matter. There is no greater stimulus towards acting in depth than this, for the reason that, paradoxically, the words of a part can sometimes become a barrier to their proper realization. When an actor is working on them in preparing his part, he can focus his entire being upon them, and in turn, the words become the magnet towards

* See page 150.

which the whole of his creative powers are directed. Before very long he can find himself 'acting the words' instead of acting what the words mean. Improvisation can be a safeguard against this, when the words of the scene are temporarily discarded and others (however bad) substituted, together of course with their appropriate action. In this way the actor's imagination is forced to work on the emotional core of the scene. When the truth of the scene is found again and thoroughly established, the original words are re-established and rehearsals resumed in the normal fashion.

Paragraphs 6 and 7 indicate perhaps an unusual awareness of the requirements of the *scene* in addition to the requirements of the part. But the point to note is again that a performer can be thinking of certain things that matter to the director and that a director can be caught out by this, if he has not thought of them himself.

Paragraphs 8 and 9 throw some light on the actor's private world, where the director can help him only very slightly. But he can be a serious hindrance if he is not aware of that world. The processes described take time, and the director must learn patience in waiting for them to happen. Nothing will hurry them to completion, but again, the proper rehearsal priorities will help.*

DURING REHEARSALS

All these processes continue during rehearsals. Also:

(10) Get familiar with other actors' faces, voices, appearances, personalities. I often try to remember their faces in detail after rehearsal, to get used to them.

(11) As far as possible I imagine that physical surroundings at rehearsals are the real set in which I shall be performing. I imagine the 'off-stage areas' to be 'real', and do so in detail, 'seeing' where I've been before each entrance.

(12) Find out how character moves, and what is the physical expression of own character.

* See Production Practice.

(13) Get character physically related to everyone and everyone of importance, on stage and off stage, if necessary.

(14) Find out who or what I am communing with at every moment of the time, either someone, or something, or myself. Or two or more things at once. If, in a play, I have to look out of a window and I listen to someone talking to me at the same time, I am conscious throughout both of the person and of the window, but in ever-shifting proportions. I must decide:

(a) What is out of the window;

(b) When the view has more of my attention than the person does, and why;

(c) Which of the two I am really more interested in.

Then I must find physical relationships with the window and with the personal relationships which will be clear to the audience.

PLAYING

(15) While playing, adjust performance to audience intuitively, without 'losing' the other actors.

(16) I must not let myself skate over bad bits, but must try to improve these on stage, and think about them off stage.

There you have a sight of the bricks with which directors build—bricks which can hardly be left to lie about in formless heaps, with neither builder nor architect. Those 'bricks' are alive, however, and that comprises what can be the director's problem, or his delight and his responsibility, according to what sort of person he is. It is not only that the actor can work intricately, with the greatest patience and skill. The fact is that he is under a self-imposed compulsion to work, and that he will do so in his own particular way whether a director is significantly present or not. He who does not realize this and who manœuvres his company without bothering to learn how they think is as pompous and foolish as the philosopher in *Rasselas*, who had to remind himself to get out of bed in time to tell the sun to rise.

Of course, not all performers will have *consciously* gone through all the steps listed above. Many, as we have seen, build up their parts intuitively, and mysterious unconscious activities are responsible in every actor for a greater or lesser proportion of the total creative process. All the more reason, then, for the director to have the thought ever before him: 'tread softly, for you tread on my dreams'. The dreams of actors can have memorable results, results which never would have happened if a director had thoughtlessly blundered into them.

I remember a particular production of The Representative, where the young actress playing one of the important parts was also used as a chorus, whose task it was to make frequent entrances and announce statistics. Each time she came on with her lacerating inventory of so many Jews deported, so many effaced from existence, she seemed herself to represent the spirit of the race at the very nadir of its history. Her appearance, normally vital and attractive, was emaciated without the help of make-up, her voice, normally resonant, had the haunting thinness of a ghost's. No better way could have been imagined in which to represent such unspeakable horrors upon a stage, yet the actress herself* merely thought she was reading out a list of numbers and categories in a reasonably detached manner. This was all the director asked of her. It is extremely doubtful whether, had he asked for the effect she actually presented, he could have achieved it. The actress was on a tightrope: on one side of it lay sentimentality; on the other, bathos. Either result would have been disastrous and either might have been possible if, in making a conscious effort to give what was wanted she had 'acted', instead of merely existing on the stage. Wisely, the director had left her to her own devices.

Dream is the fine matter of theatre, the rare ether from which drama is made, as the planets are formed out of

* Barbara Barnett in The Representative by Hans Hochhuth, directed by John Harrison (Birmingham Repertory Theatre, 1966).

nothingness. The imaginations of writers, of actors and directors too are part of that ether, and all have a part in the mystery of theatre. It is when the balance between these three goes wrong that the magic fails to work. Magic, it is true, is not fashionable at the present time. And the kind of balance of which I write is absent from the contemporary theatre often enough. Much of the stuff of today calls for a director-dictatorship which, in order to take on the task of making the material at all theatrically presentable, must more than ever lose its own sense of proportion. Whatever the value of a piece such as *Marat–Sade*, it cannot be doubted that it wastes the skills of the actors to whom it gives employment: the only skills necessary to the writhings and mouthings that are its chief activity are those of an immaculate technical expertise, which it may give great personal pleasure to a director to juggle about with. There can be no duality in this. The disease, moreover, is catching: the current fashion can misuse actors even more: when professional actors are made to encapsulate their personalities within gigantic carnival heads while they scrawl obscenities on the walls of the stage* in the name of 'Satire' and the theatre's service of a social purpose, the ultimate degradation of the actor has arrived.

But it is too easy (if one forgets one's own sense of those values which endure, if in fact one forgets history) to regard certain aspects of the present theatrical scene with sadness. It seems bad when dramatists, the prime movers of theatre creativity, turn their backs on such things as the expression of thought and the shape of emotion, when they make a lewd face at their heritage of argument and imagination and poetry. It seems equally bad when the leaders of the acting profession, who should be concerned with its progress and purpose, fail to take a responsible interest in those who are coming after them. One's sadness and scorn could bubble over at the sorriest sight of all, that of the distinguished worshipping the

---

* *America Hurrah*, first presented in an off-Broadway theatre, and subsequently at the Royal Court Theatre, London, in August 1967.

immature, for fear of growing old (for that is how a bad fashion can live beyond its reasonable span).

Such easy negative thoughts must be resisted. A director is positive or he is nothing. Michael Tchehov, a beloved acting teacher who must have inherited many of his uncle's qualities, used to tell his students a truism which everyone should remember. 'Never', he said, 'never let yourself be affected by what you may think is bad about your fellow actors. Concentrate on what you know is good and from this your own good will grow.' Such is the thinking of many younger actors, and these find time to interest themselves in those that are younger still. As for the prime movers, we need merely two or three dramatists to turn up who have something worth saying and know how to say it,* and balance in the theatre world can be back where it belongs. Meanwhile the playhouses of the world continue to present Shakespeare and Tchehov and Anouilh and Shaw and Ibsen and Strindberg and Pirandello and Congreve and Molière, O'Neill and O'Casey and the hosts of the great writers who have given artists something to get their teeth into. Here are the priceless treasure-chests of theatre.

The actor holds one of the keys which can open any of them.

The director who has what Stanislavsky called the 'feeling of true measure' holds the other.

---

* Perhaps Peter Nichols is one of these. For all its 'modern' technique and shattering outspokenness, A Day in the Death of Joe Egg is deeply rooted in human feeling and character, and provides both actors and director with opportunities to express the gamut.